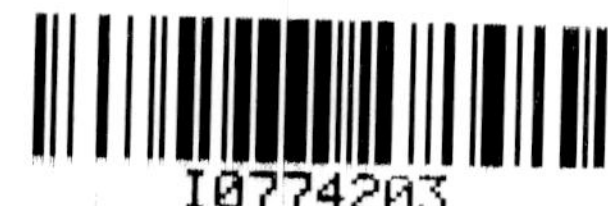

May each color you choose illuminate your adventure in this magical world of discoveries and dreams. Let's color life with joy!

Cinthia Santana

2024

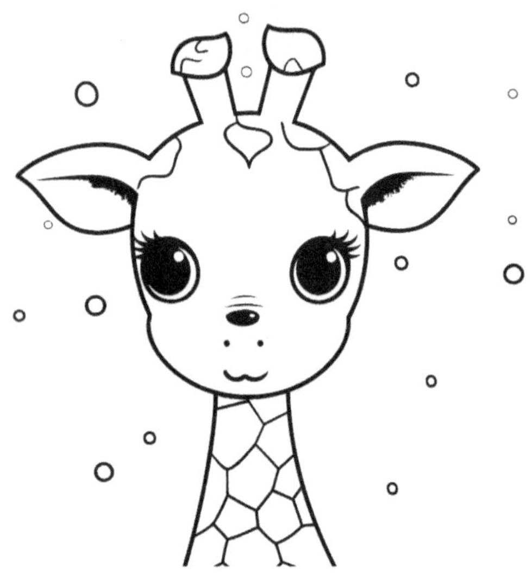
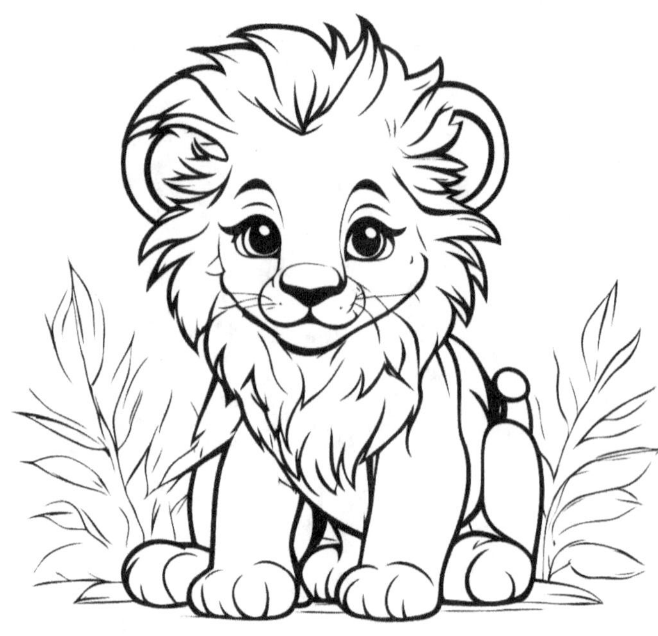

This Book Belongs to:

____

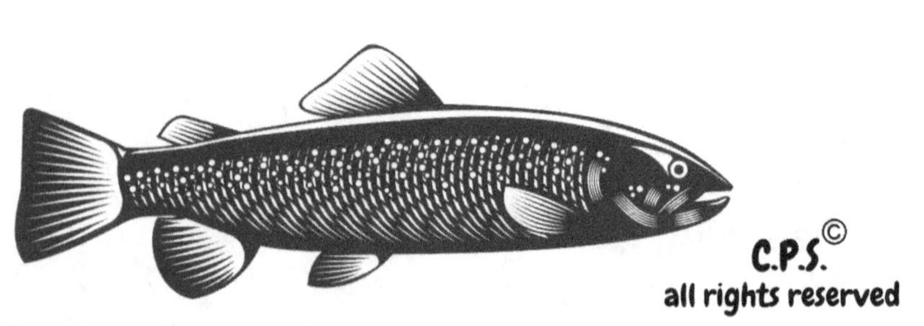

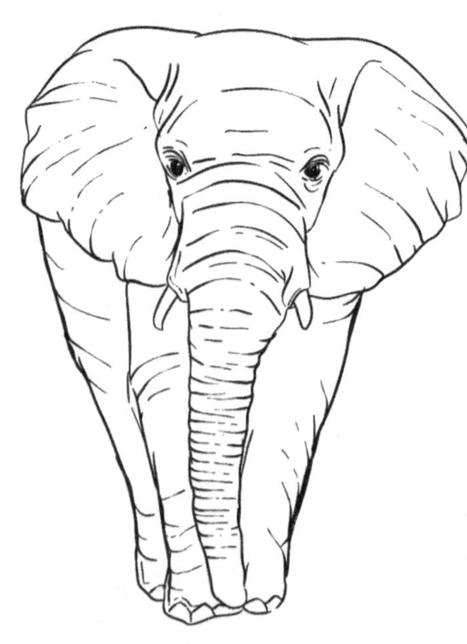

Test Color Page

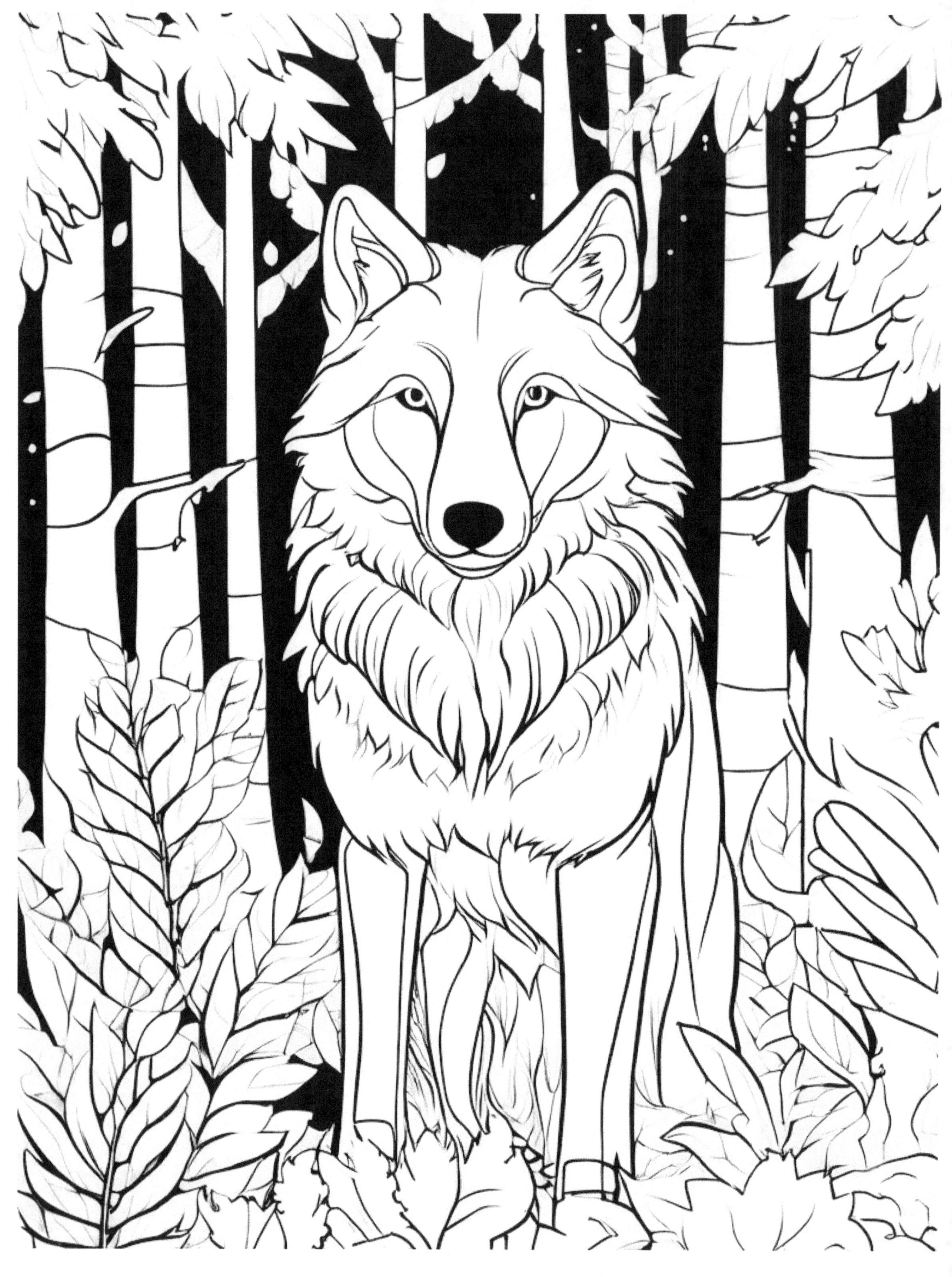

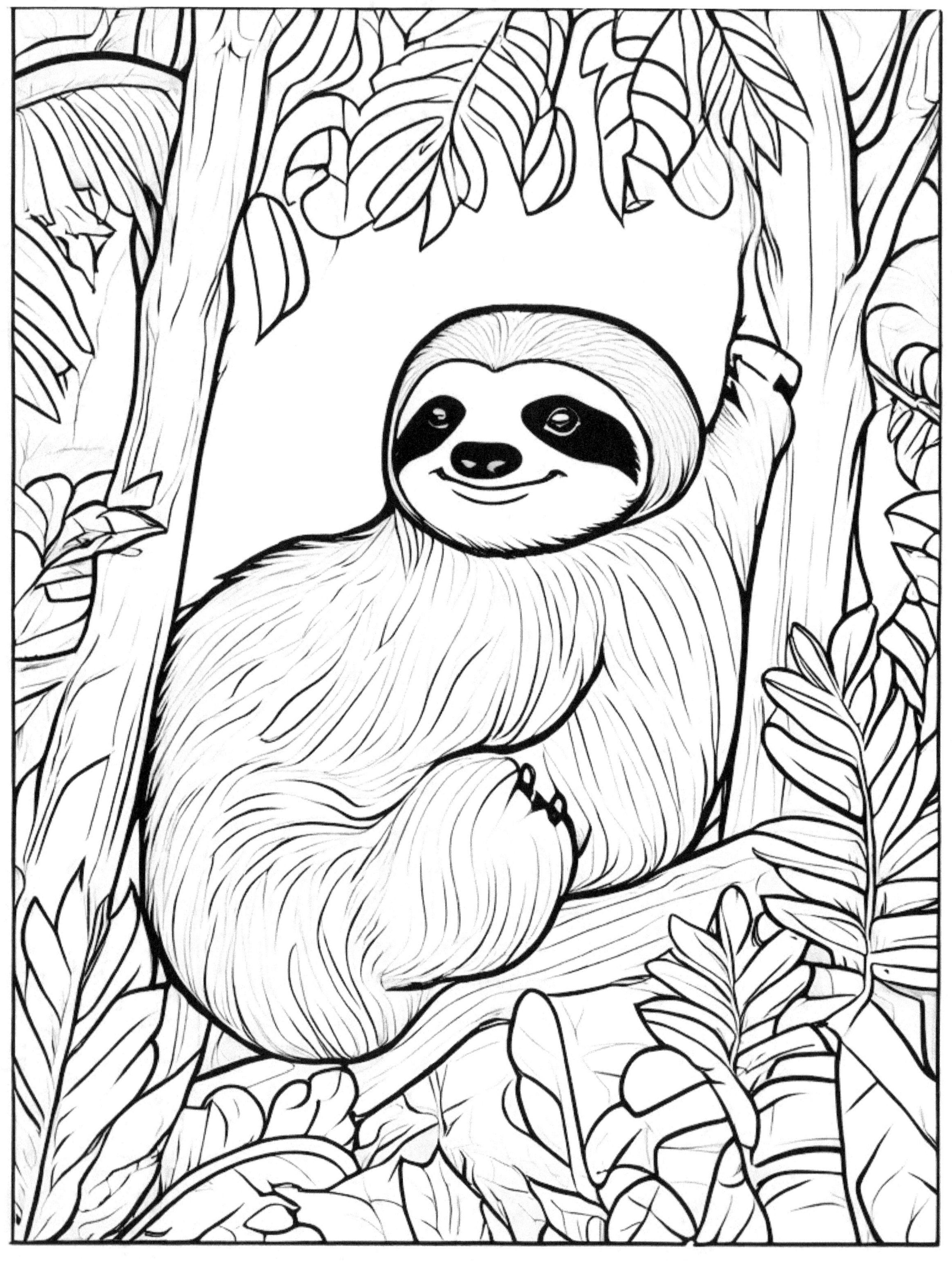

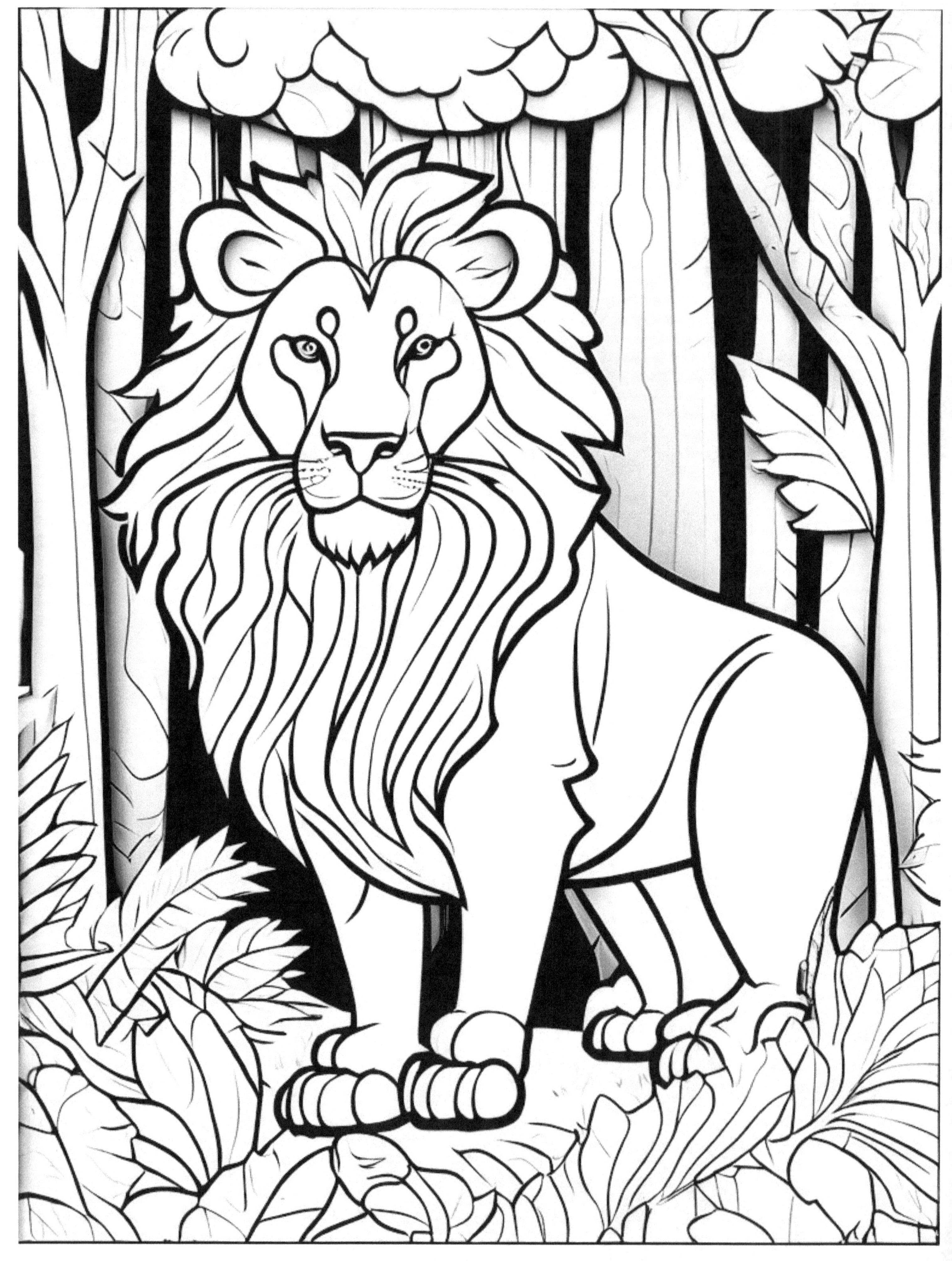

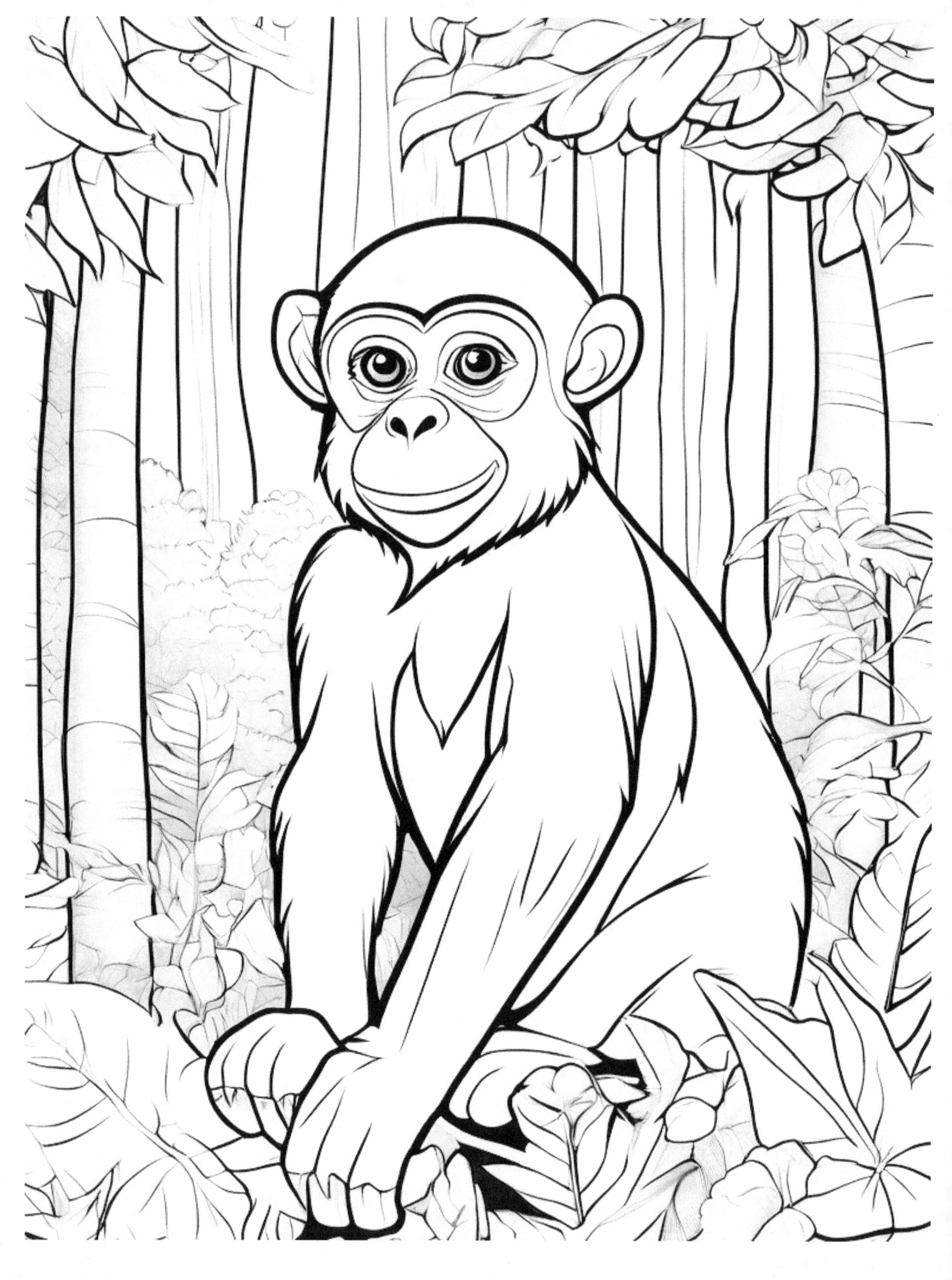

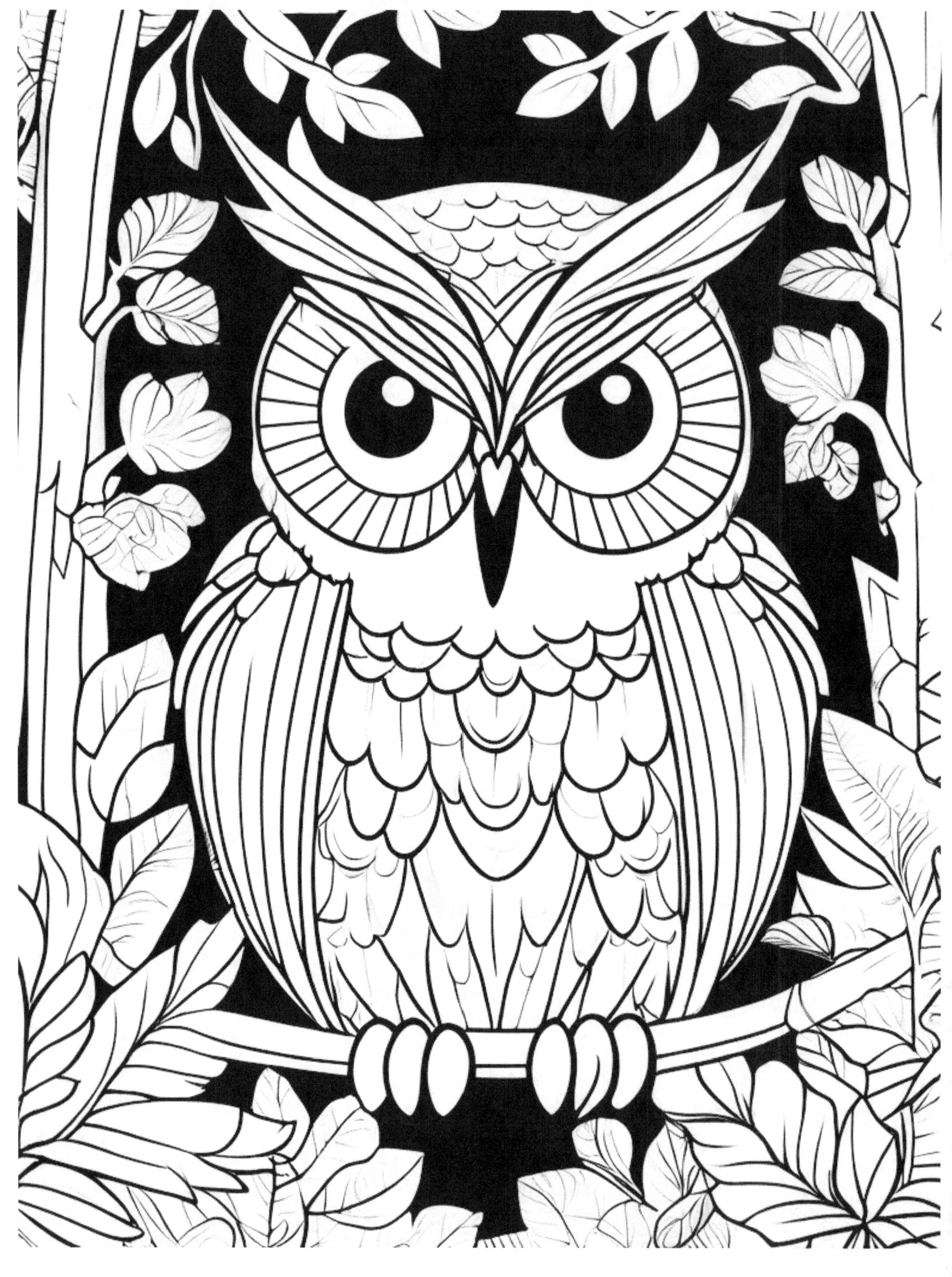

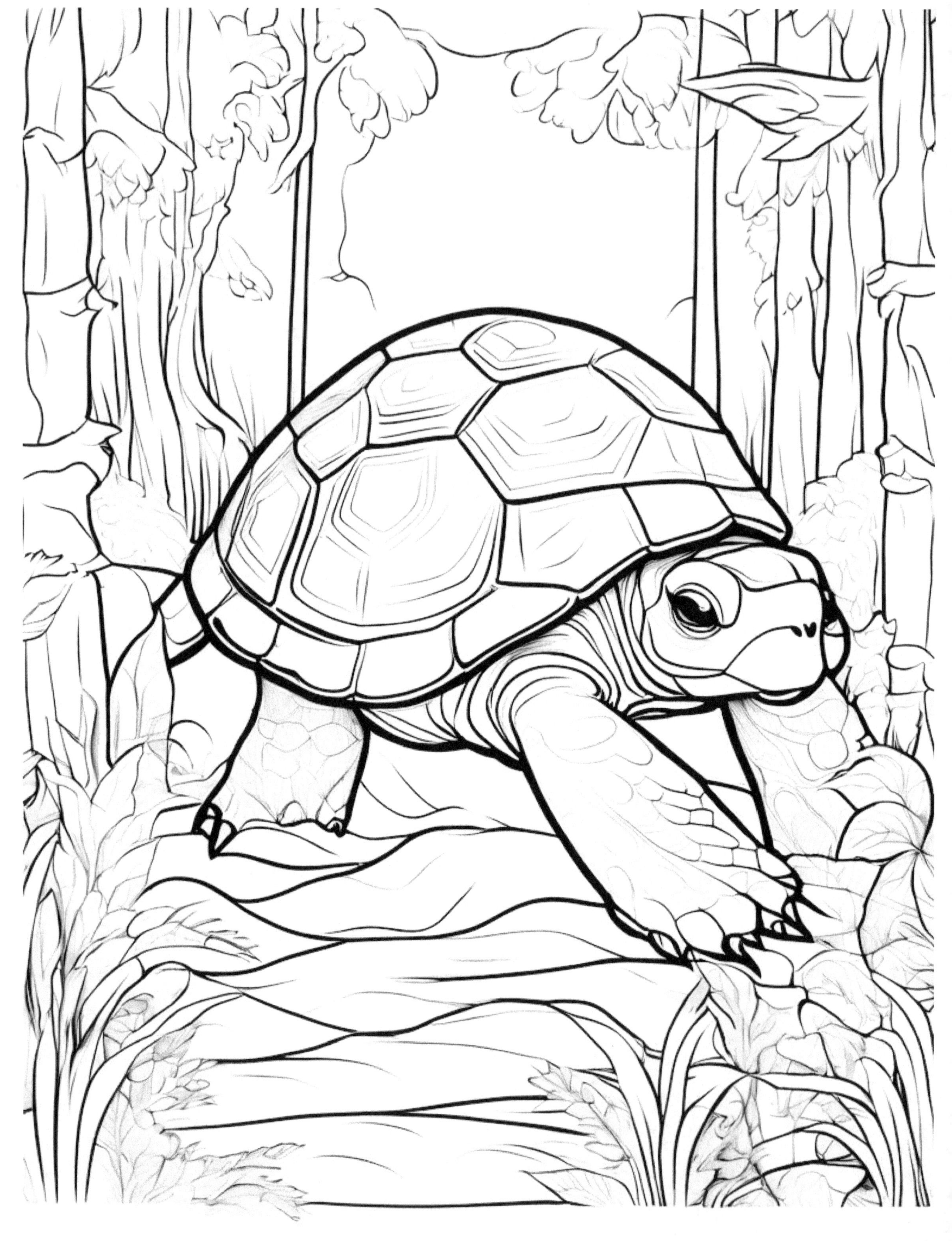

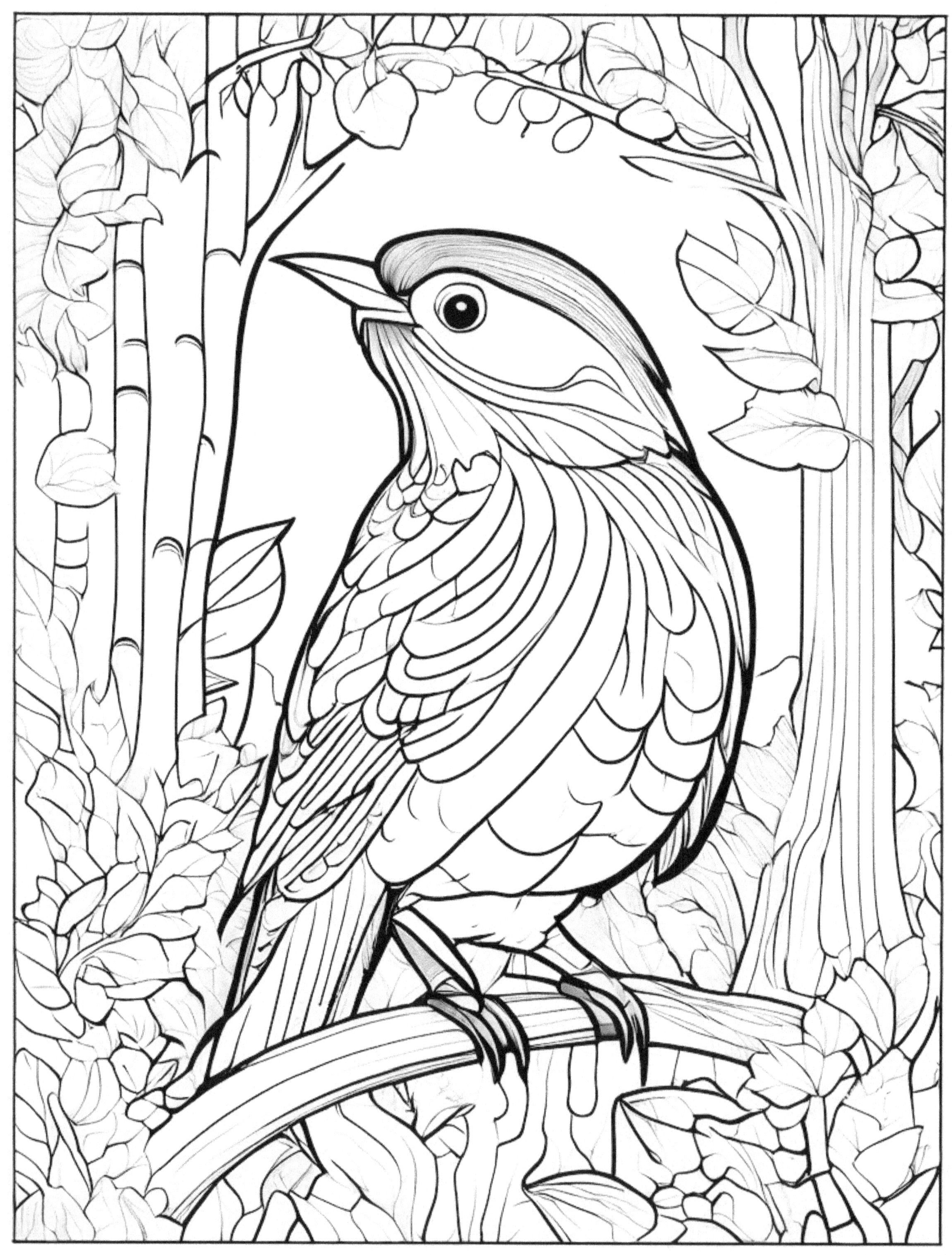

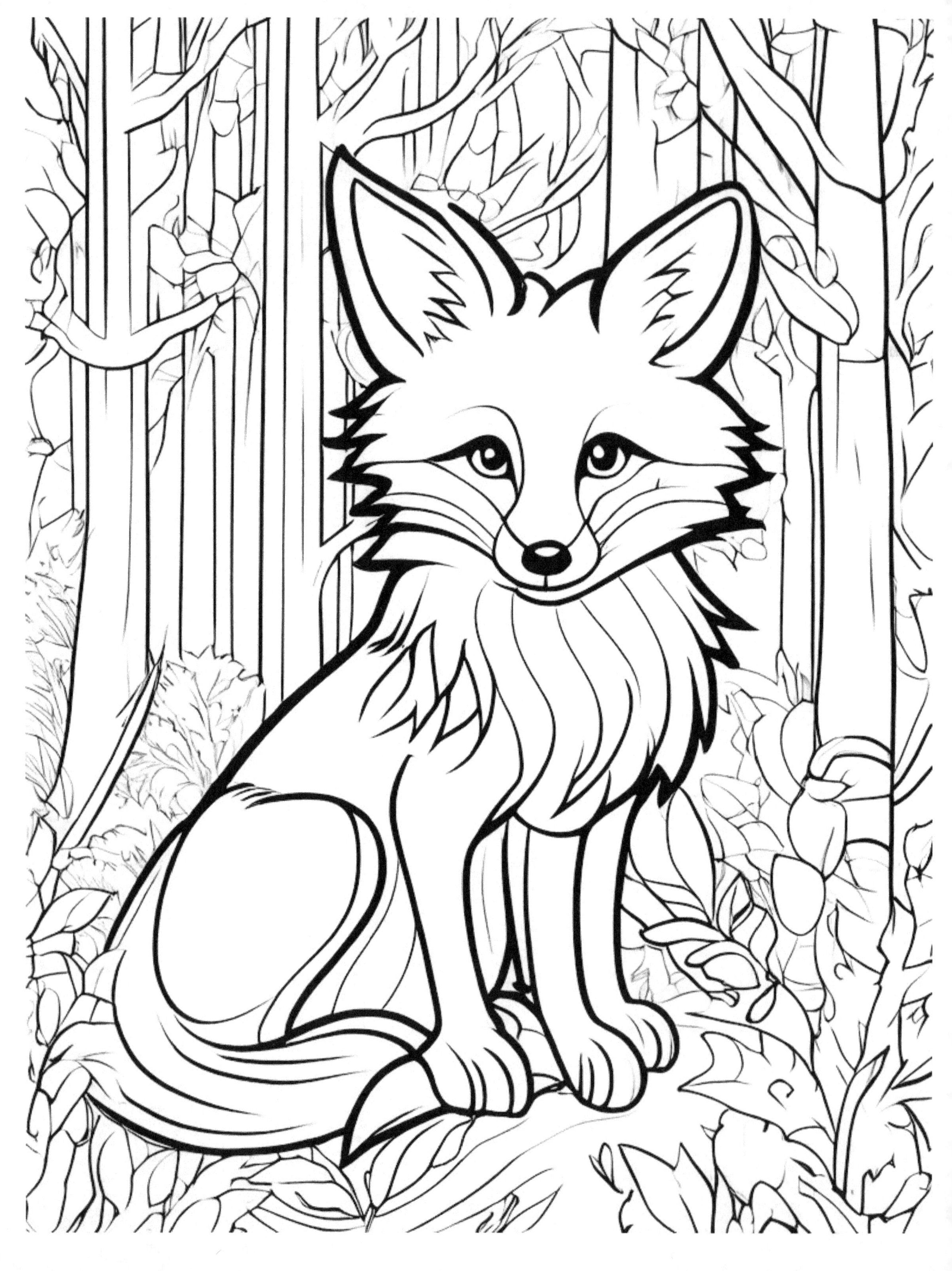

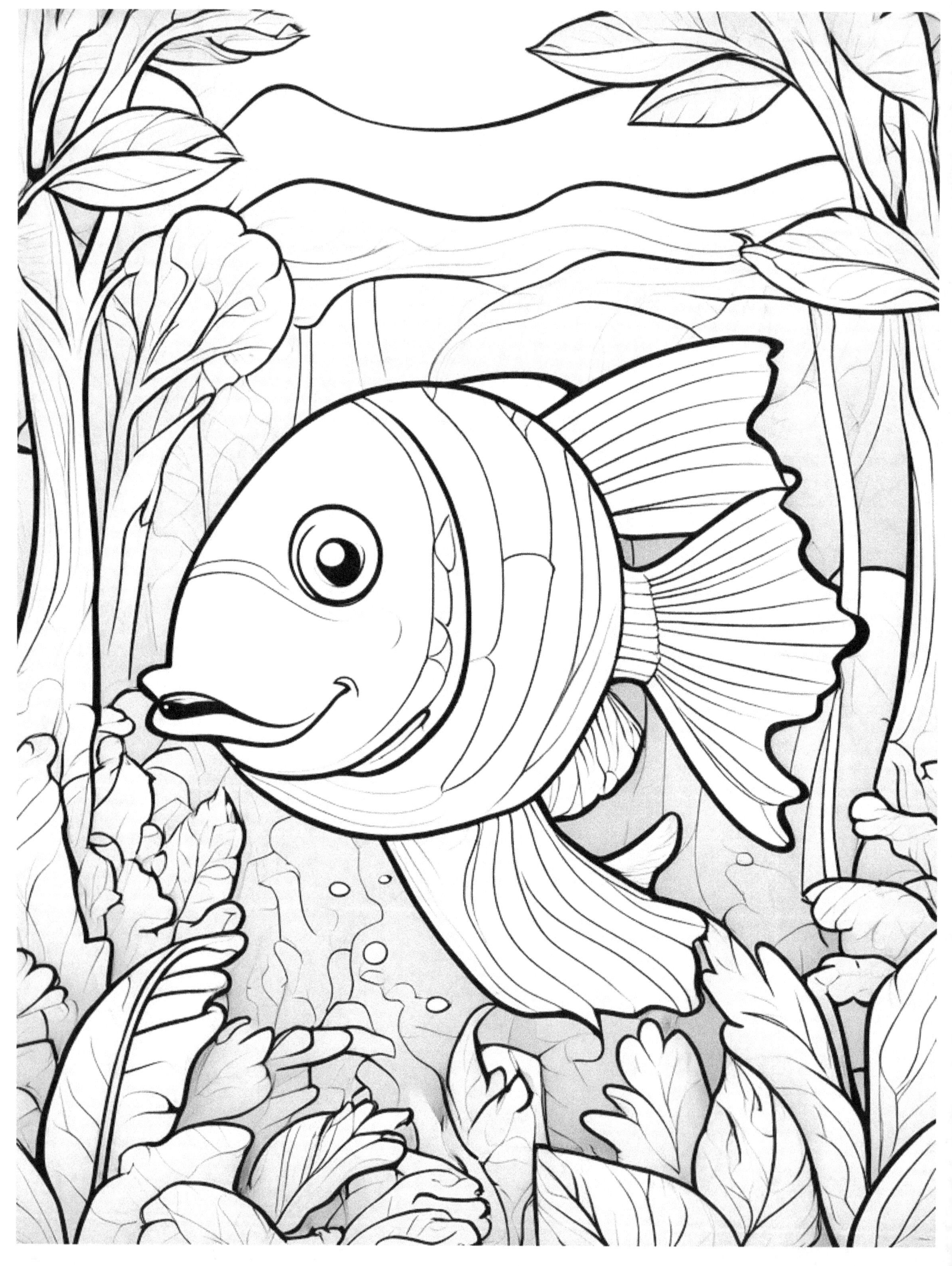

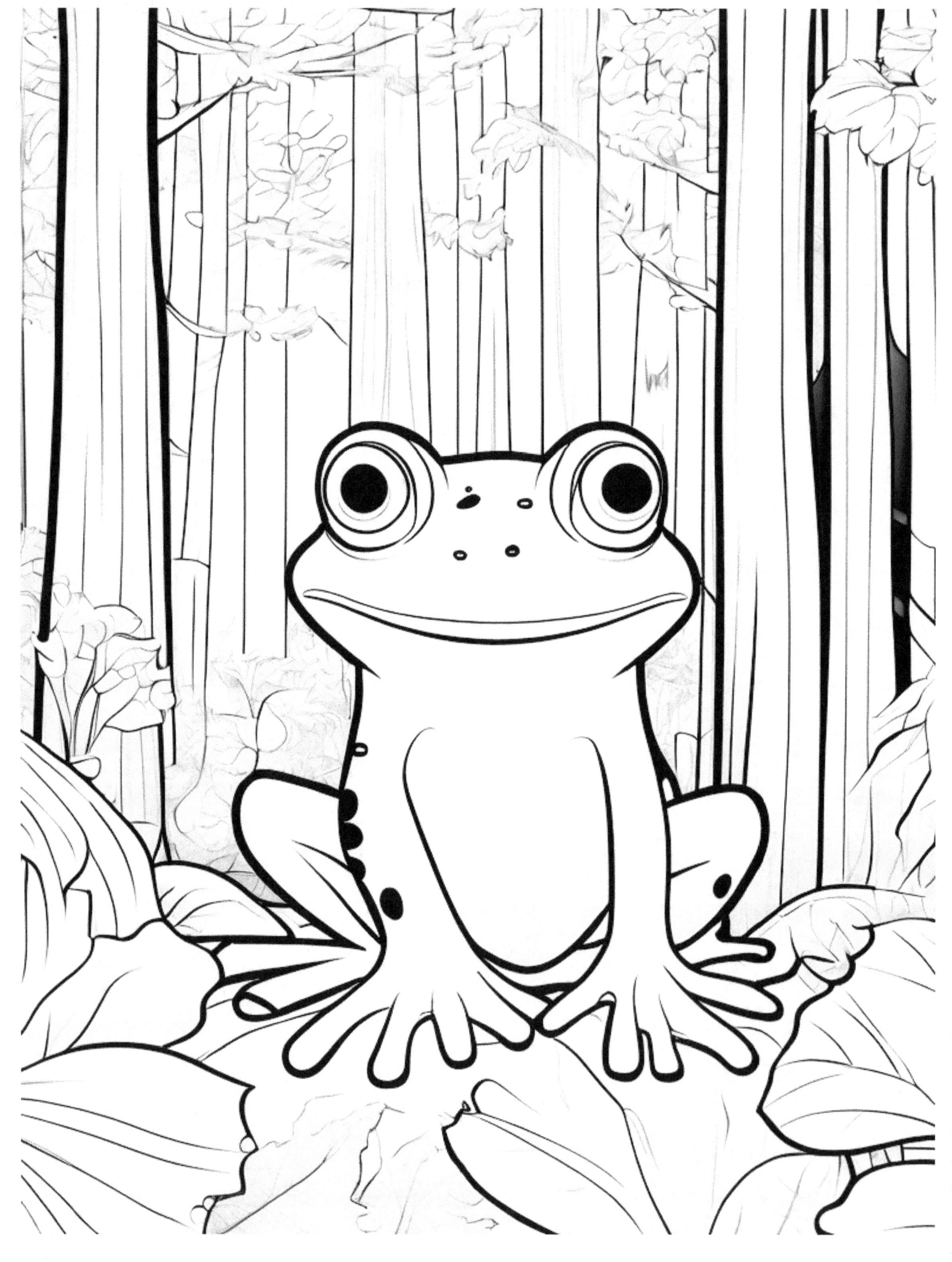

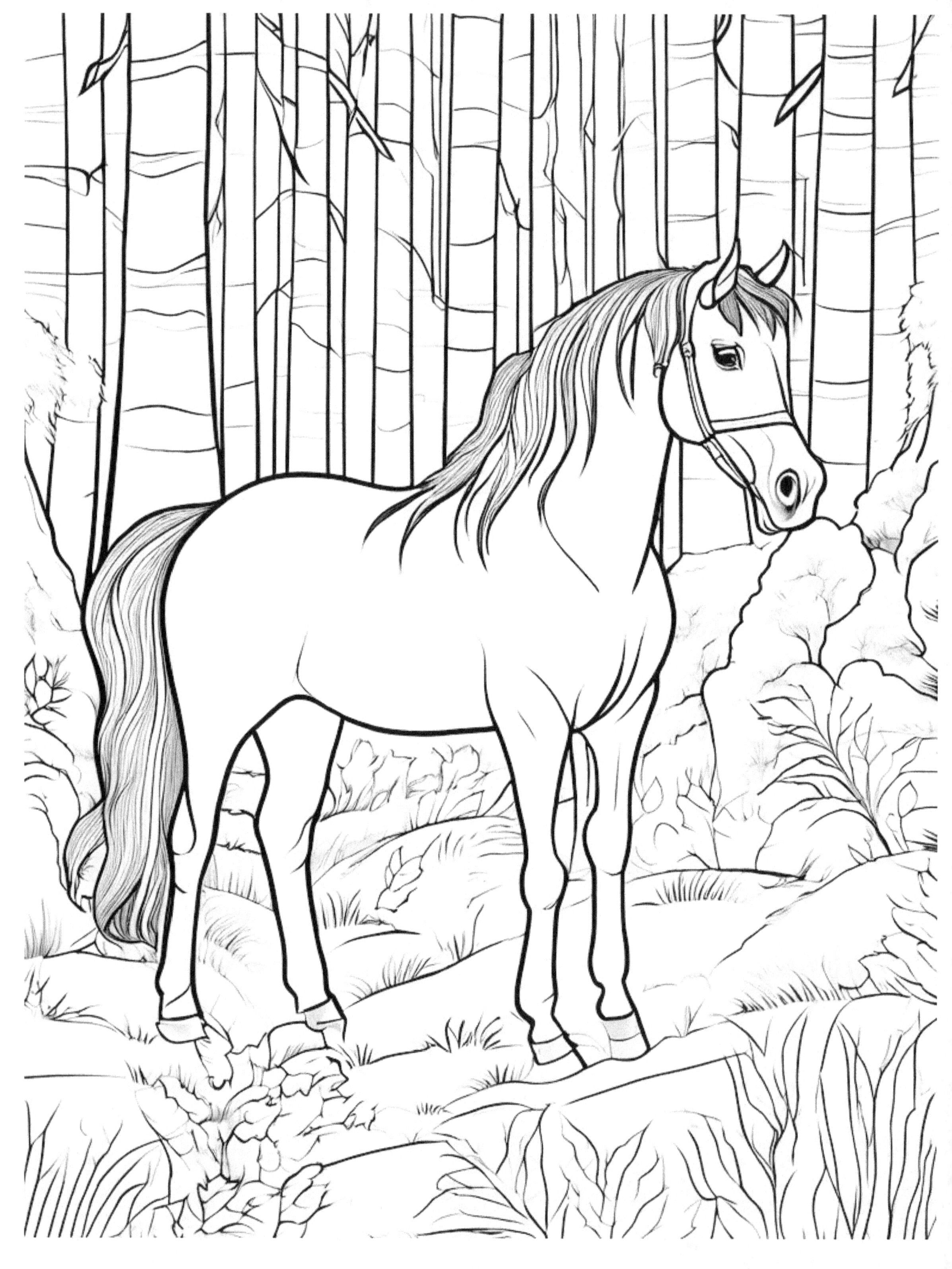

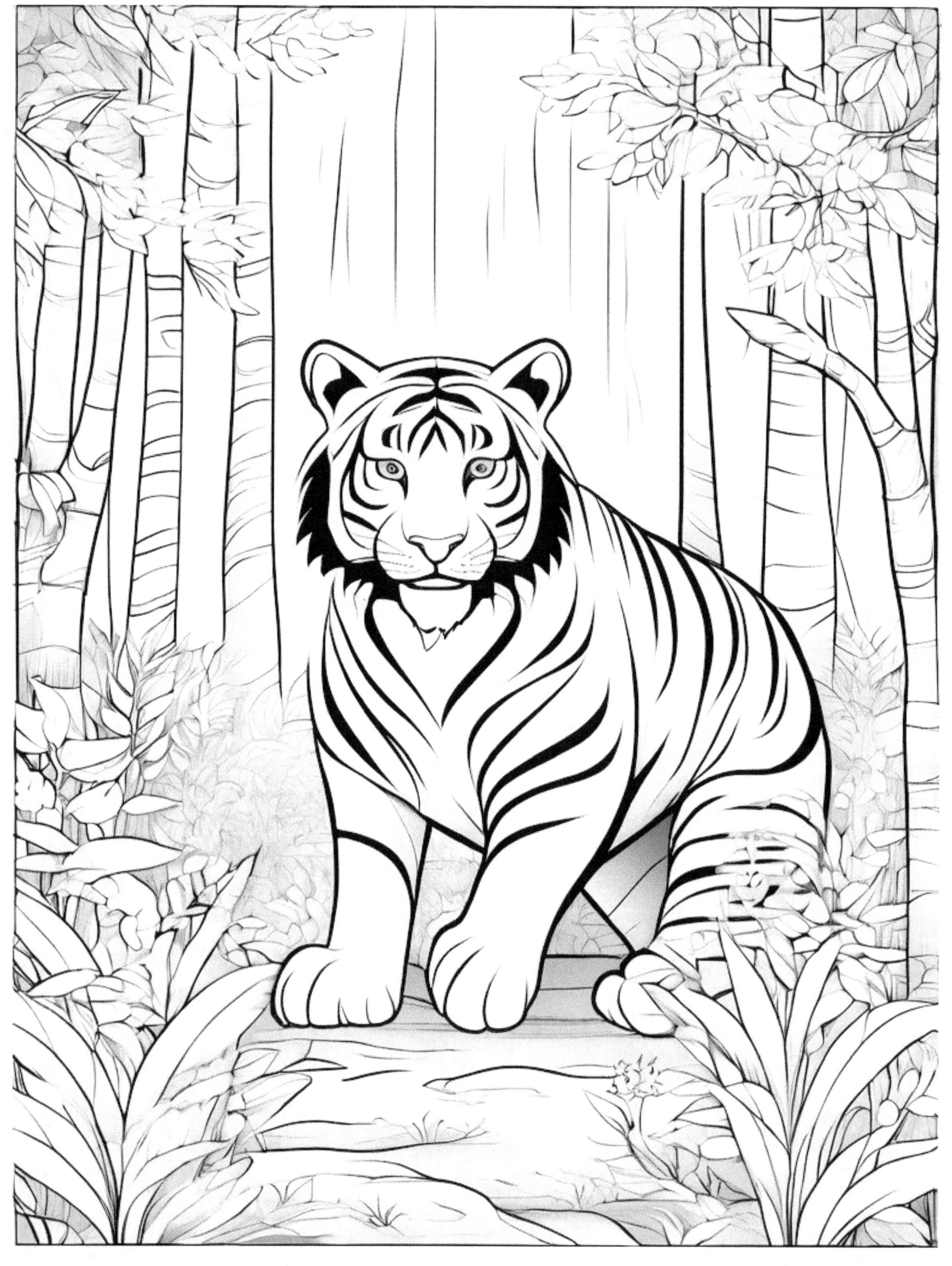

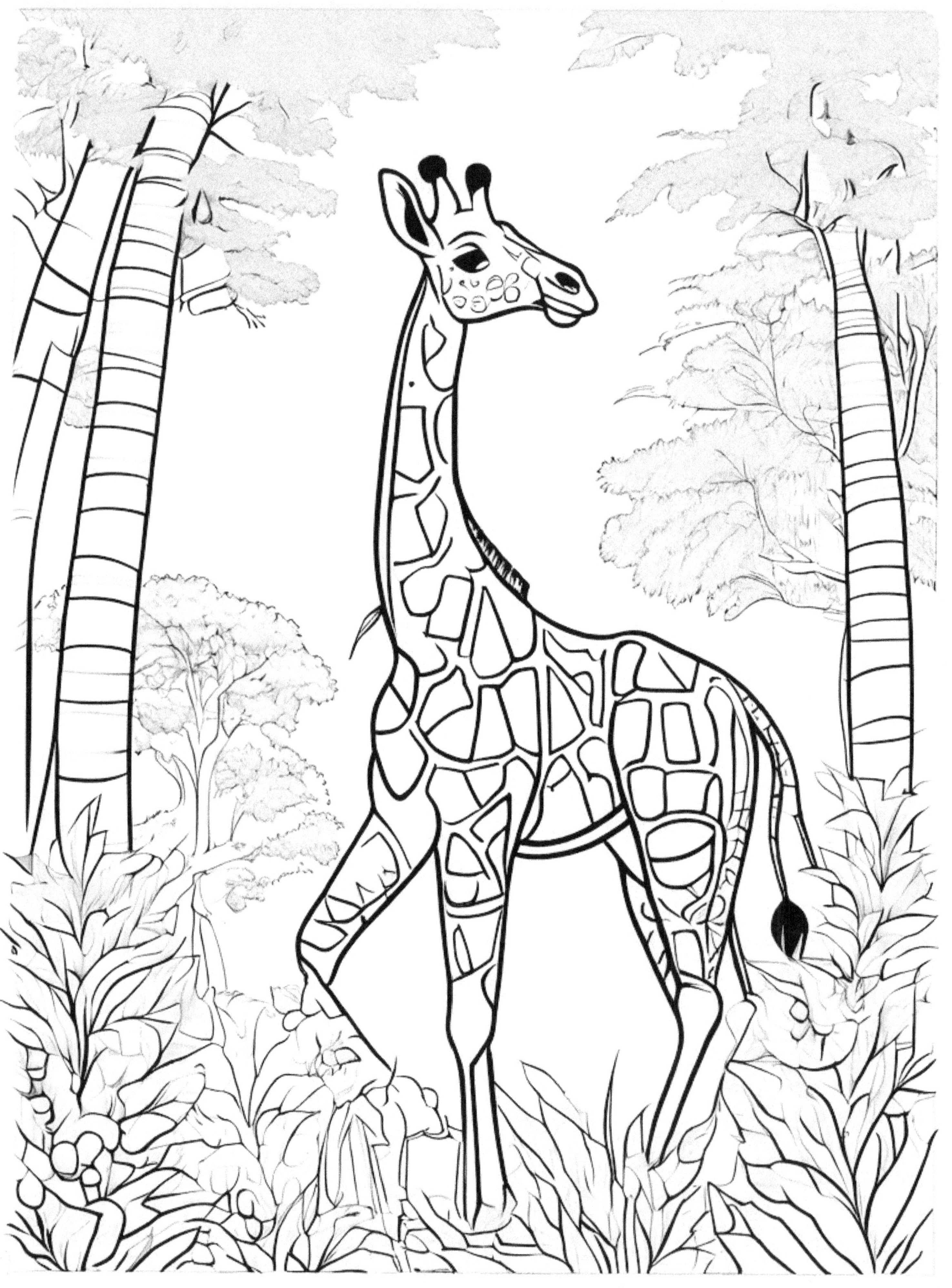

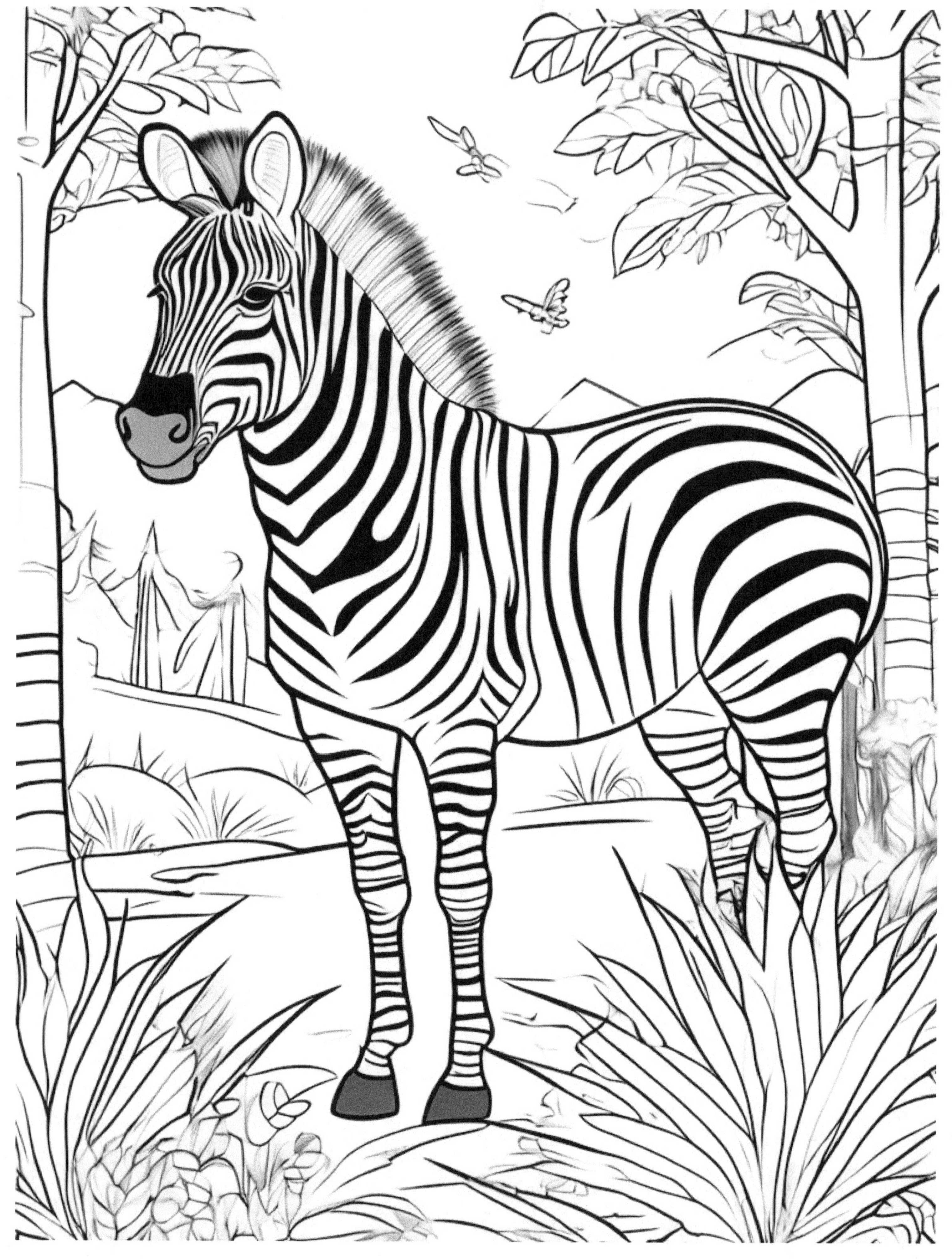

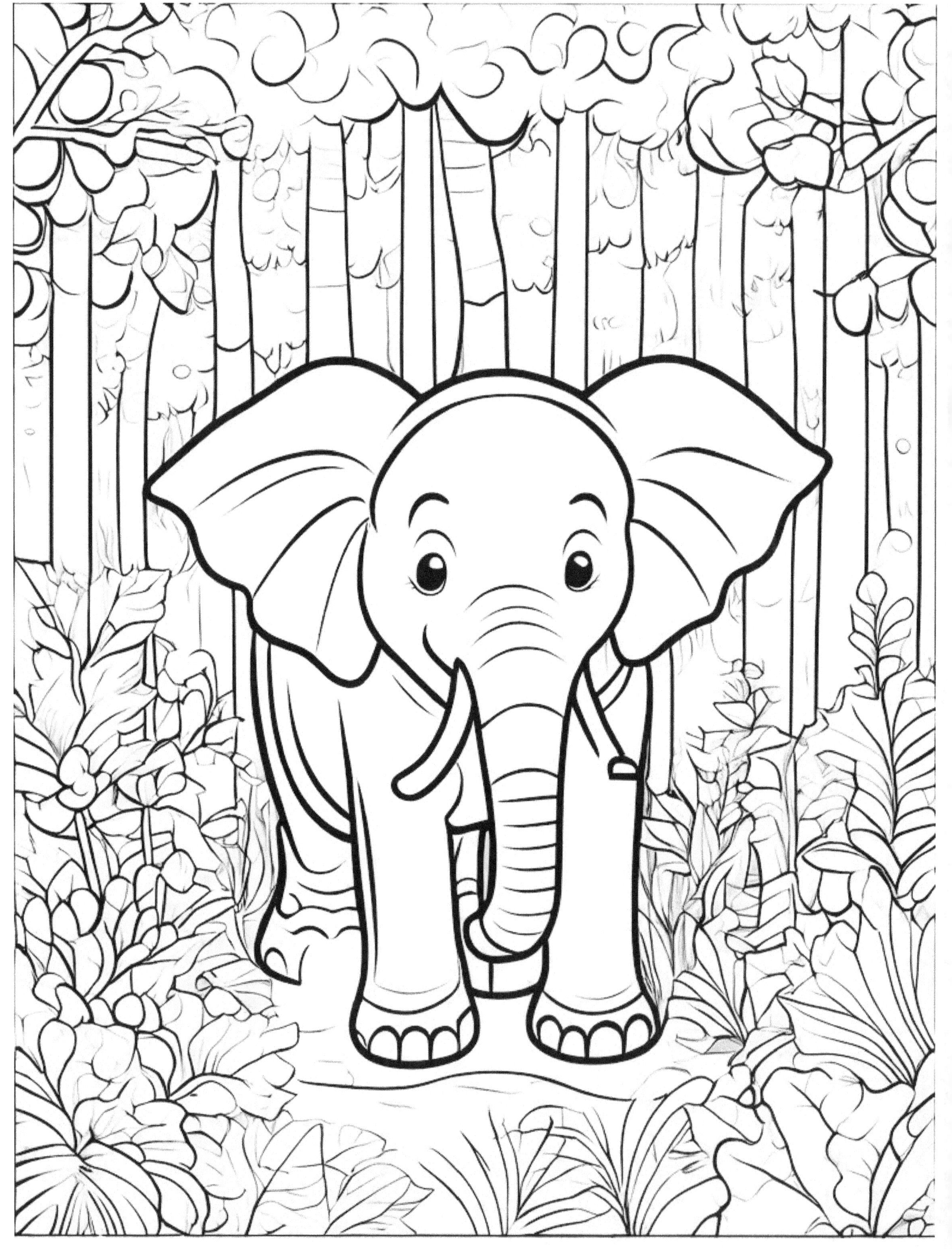

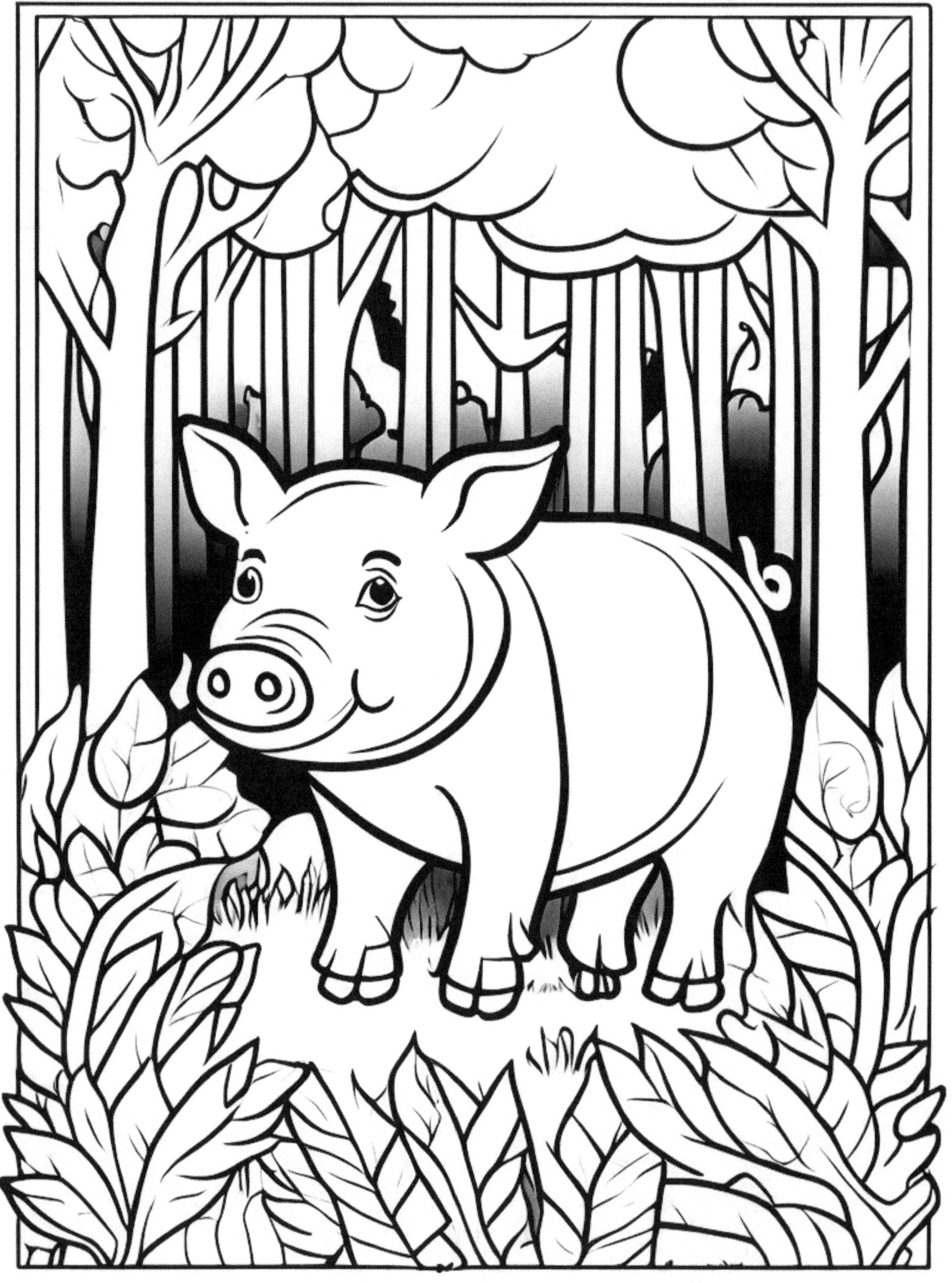

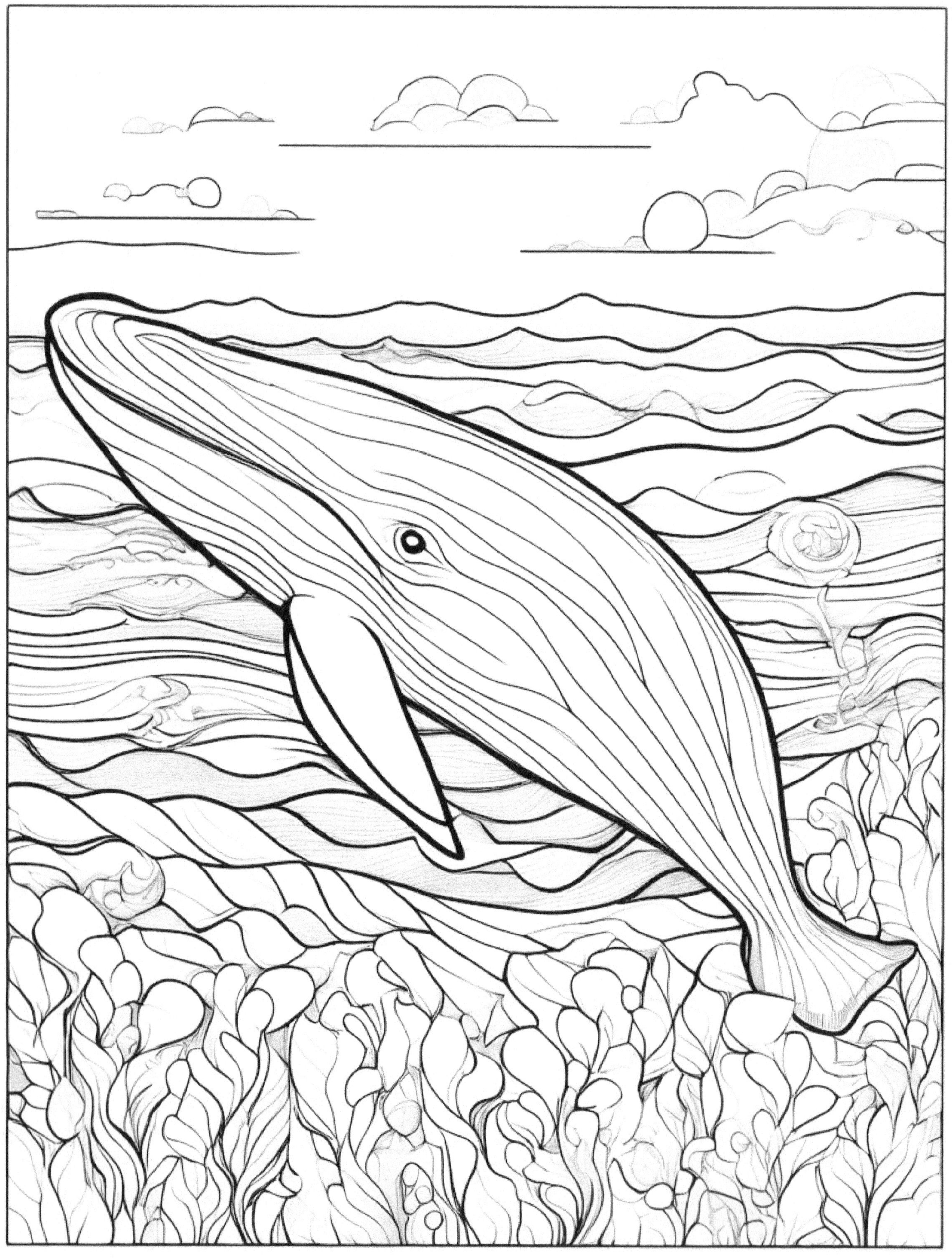

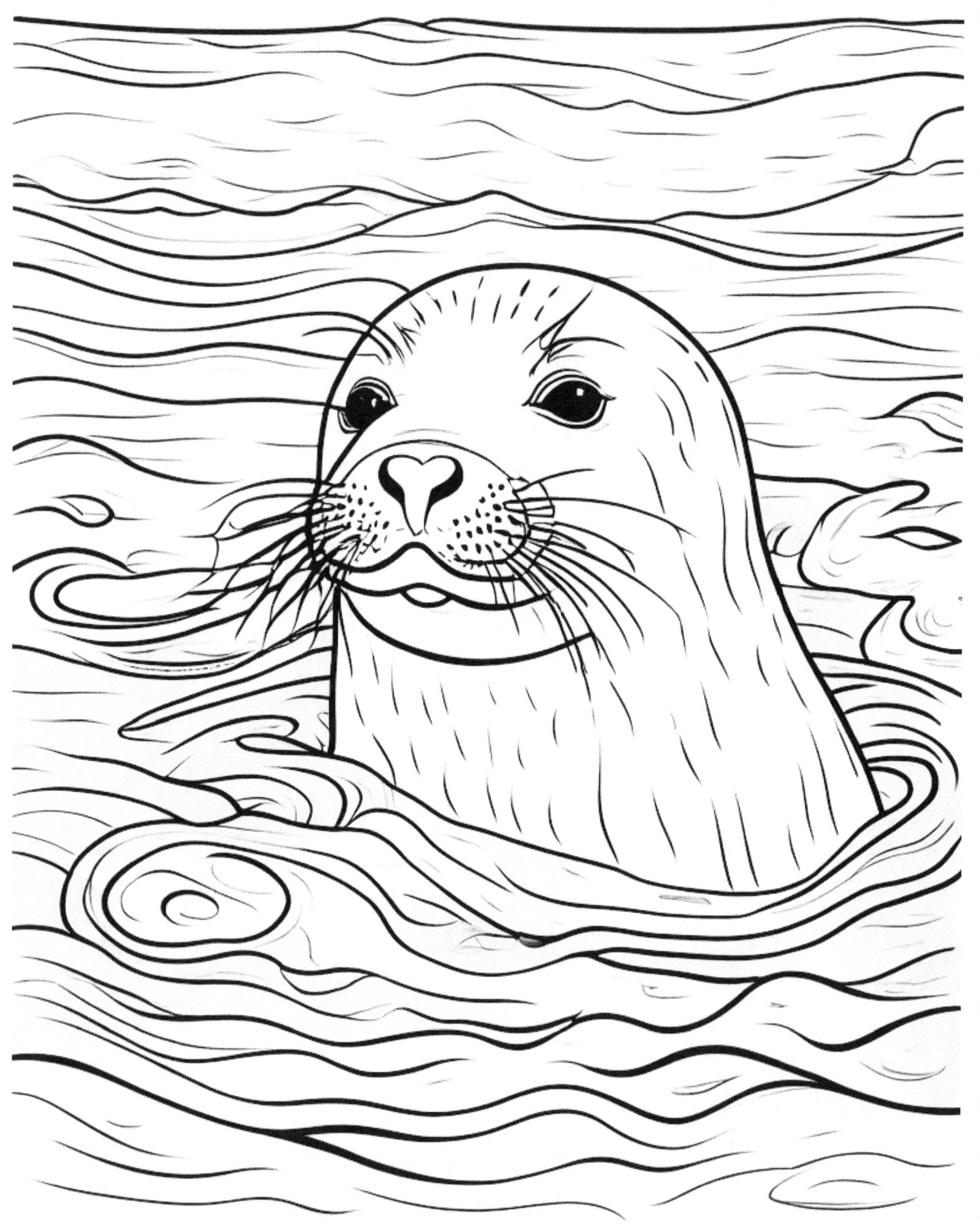

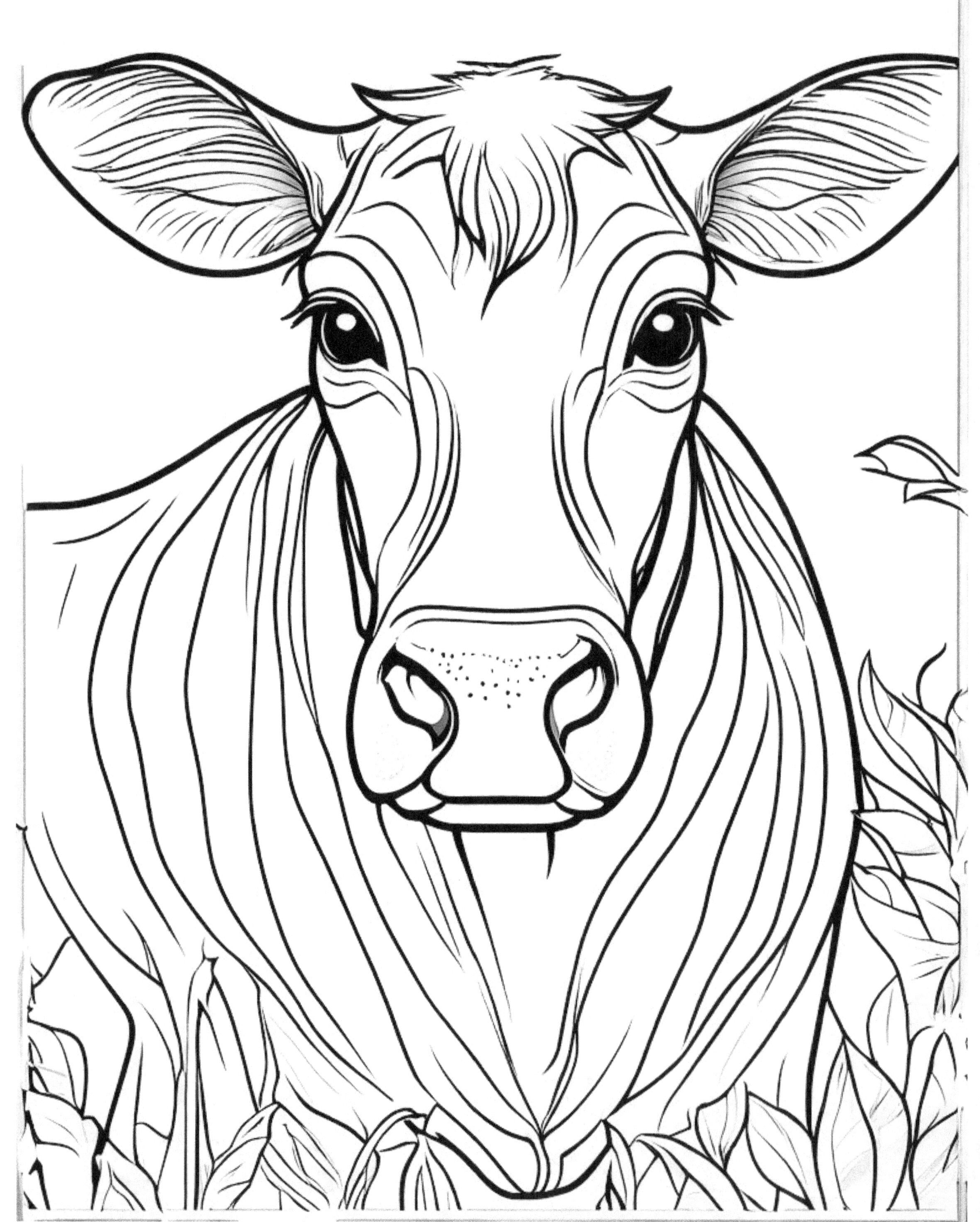

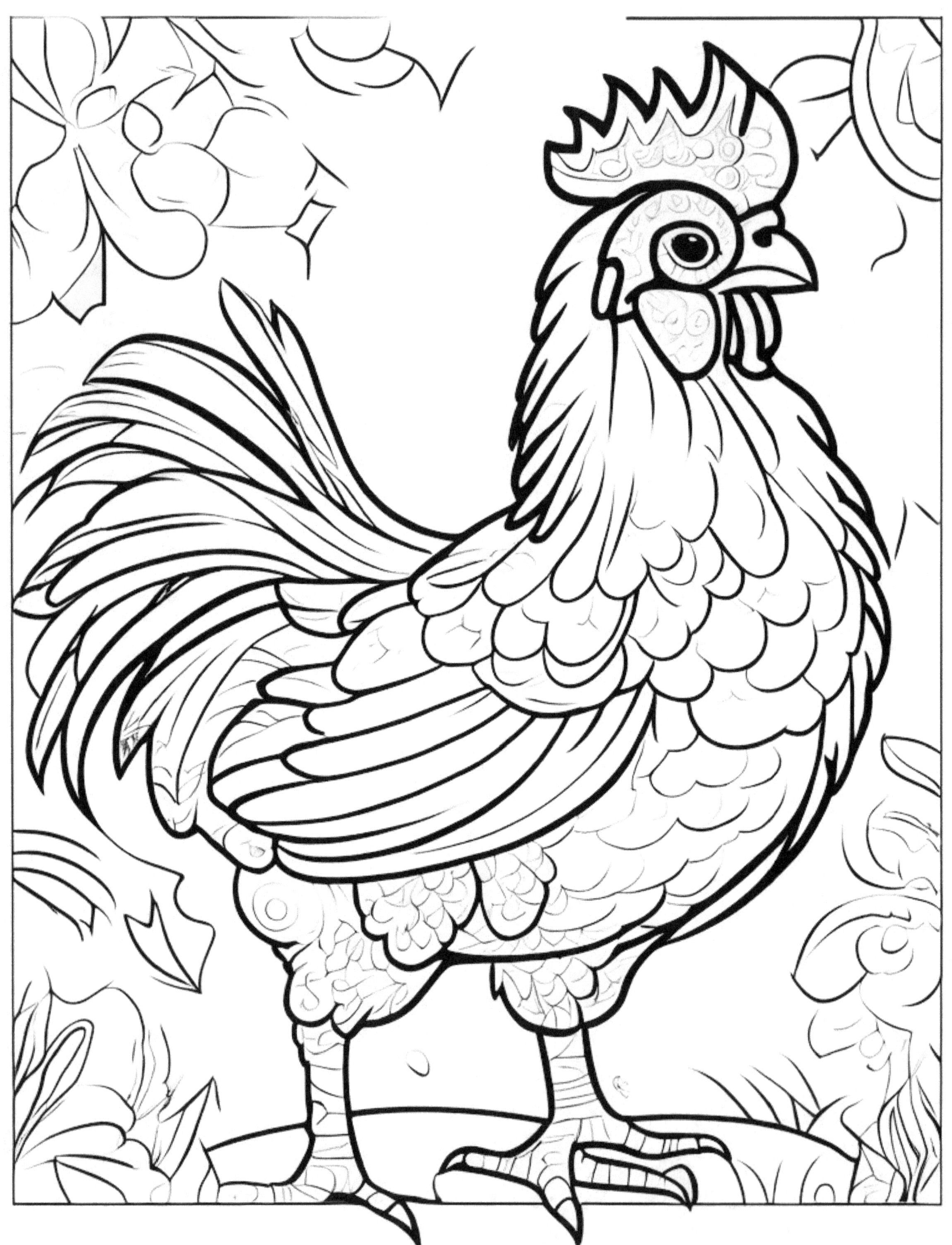

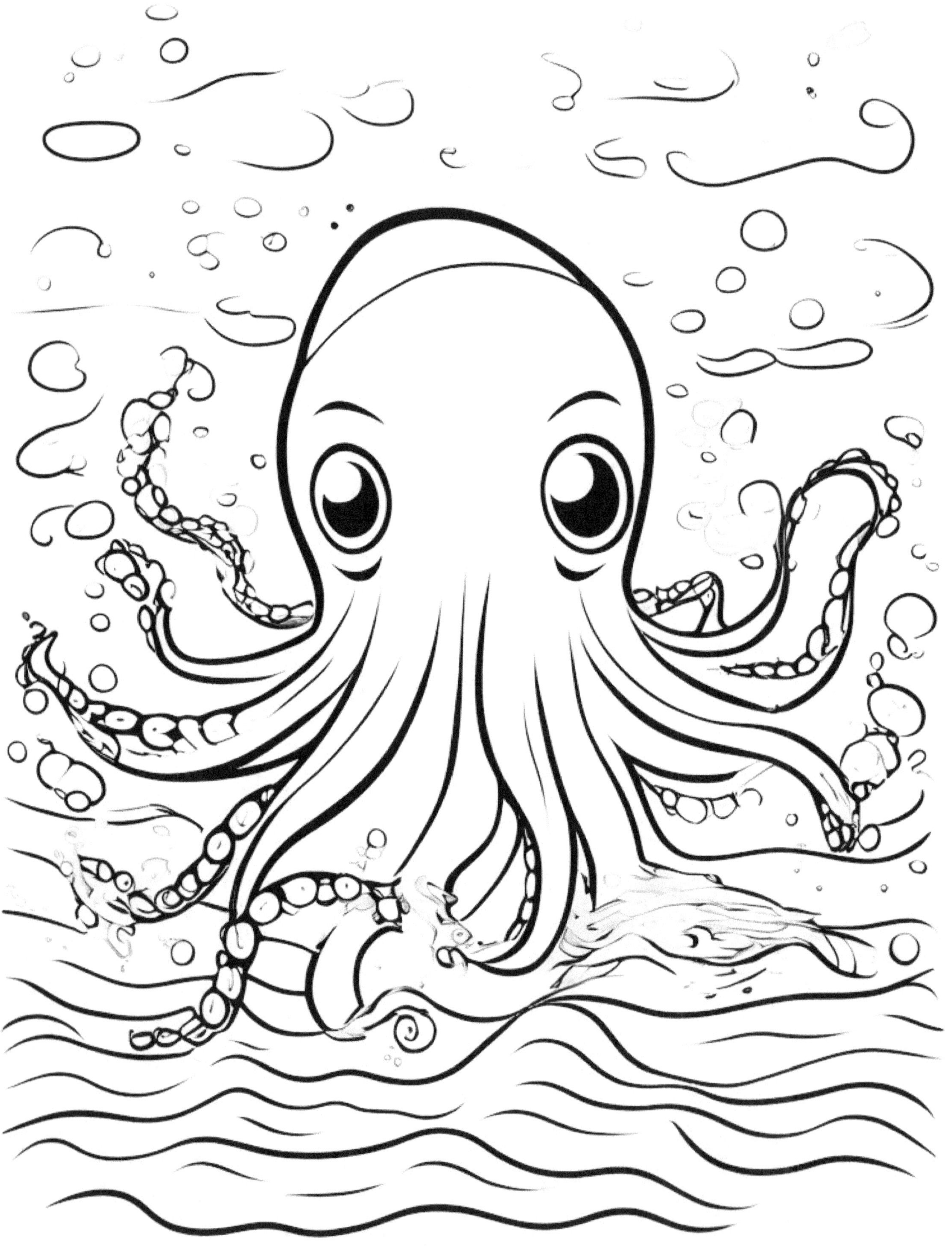

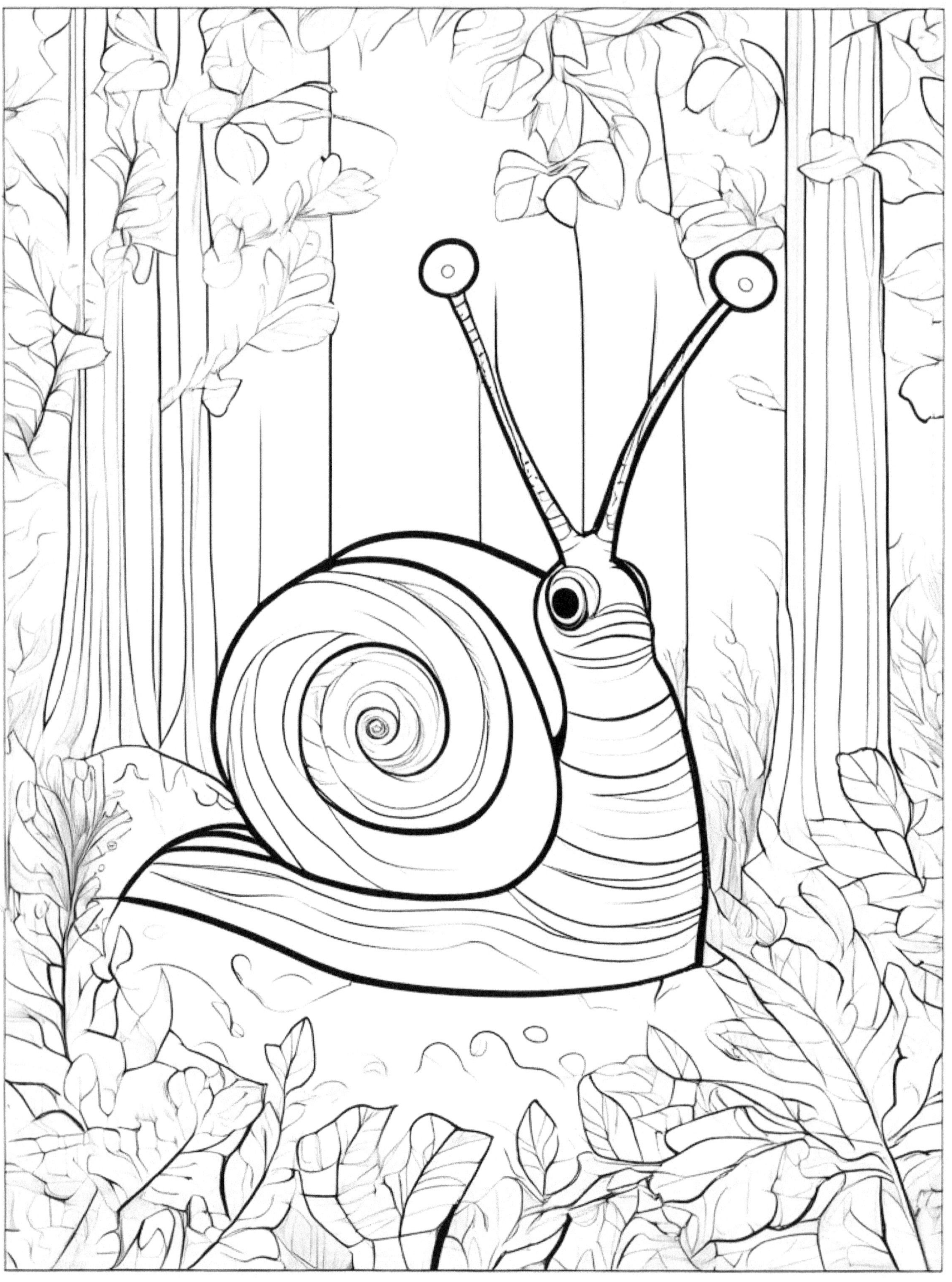

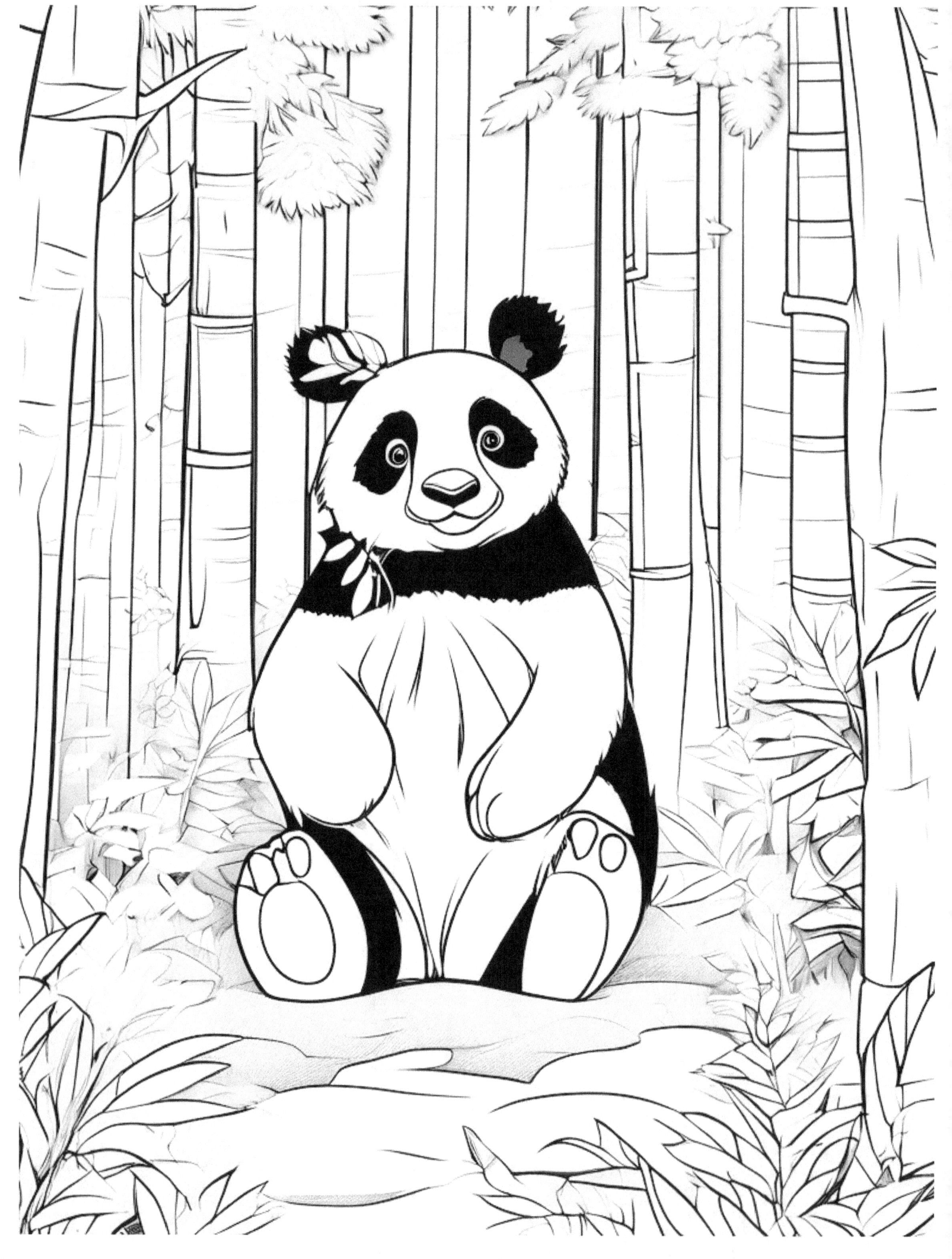

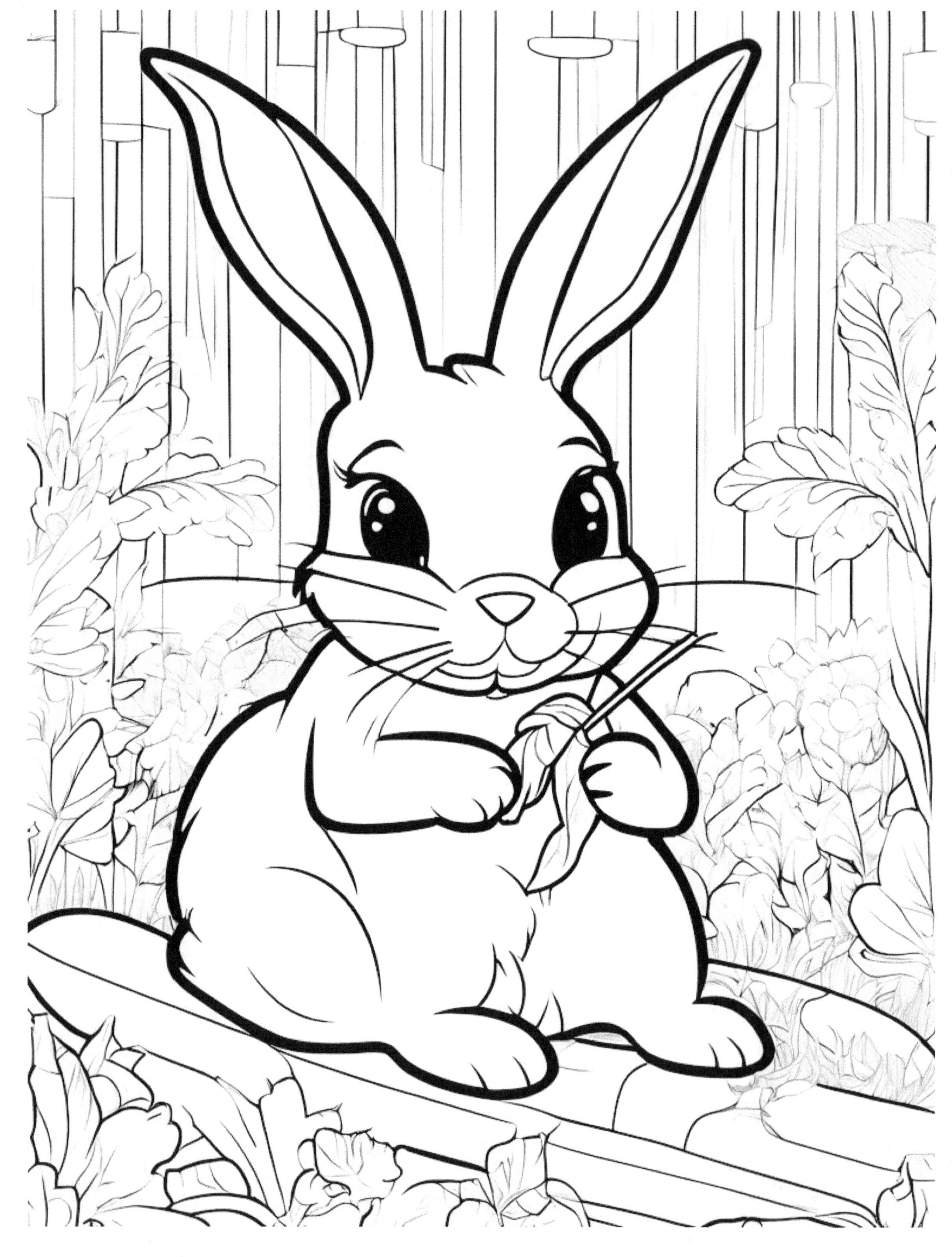

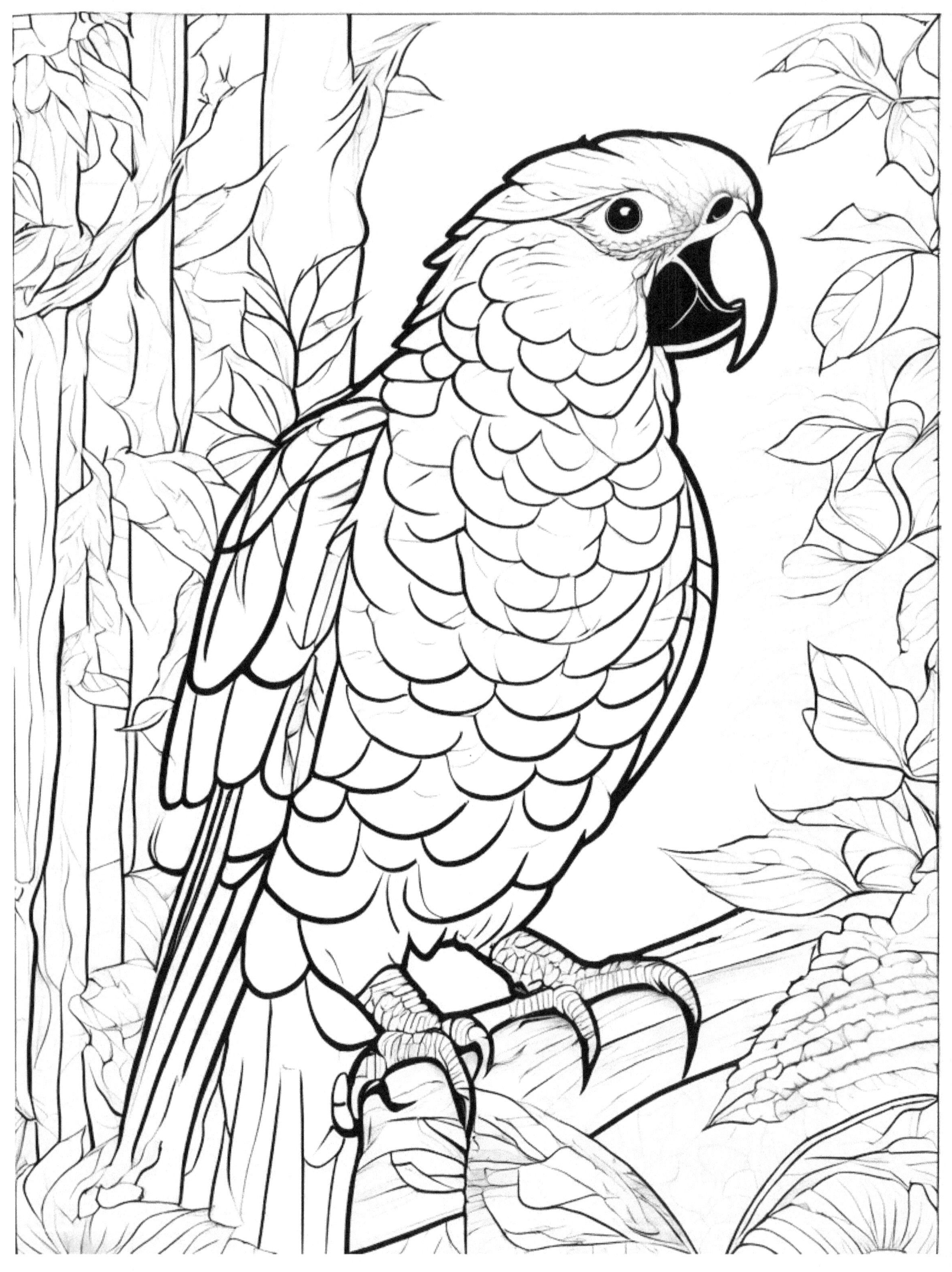

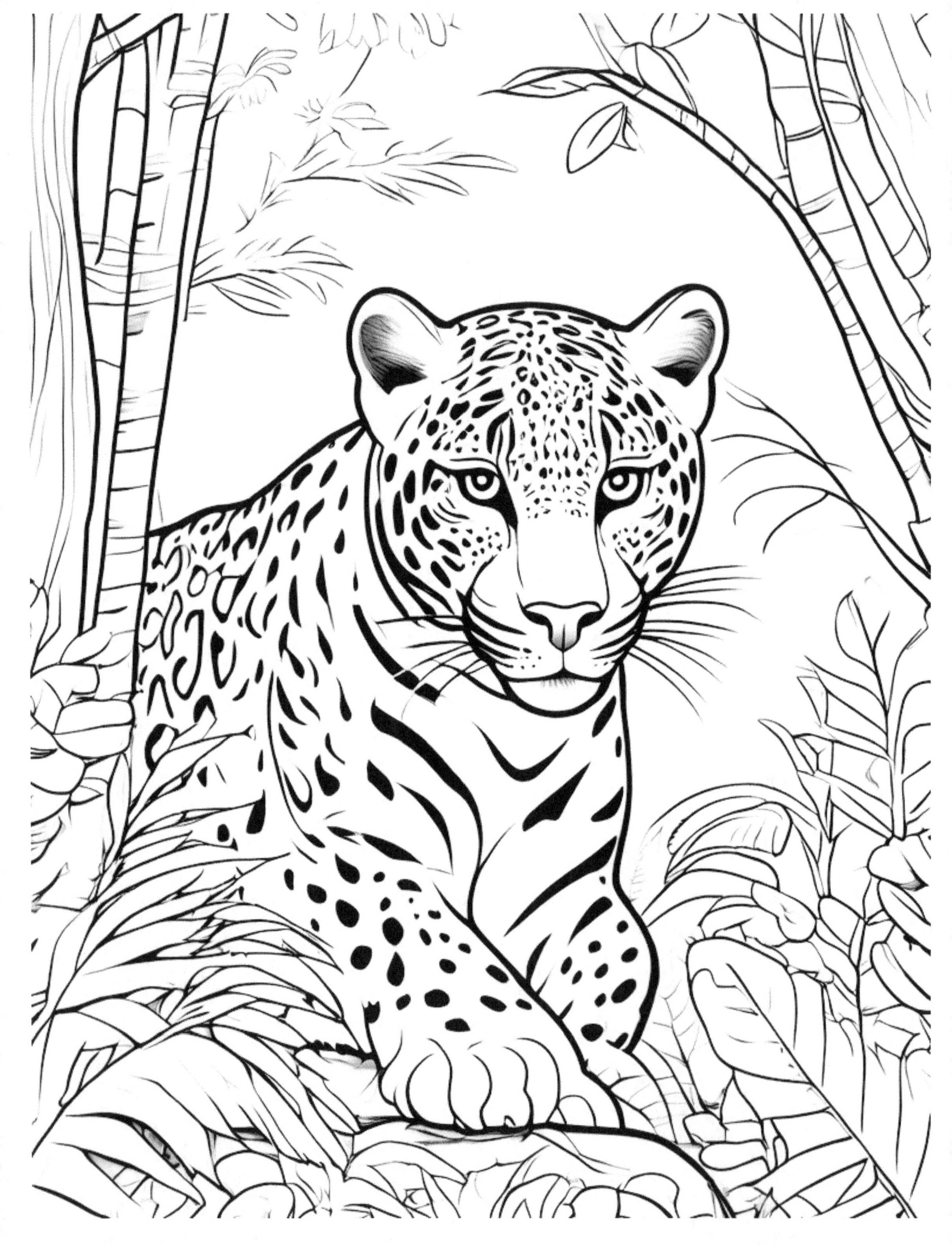

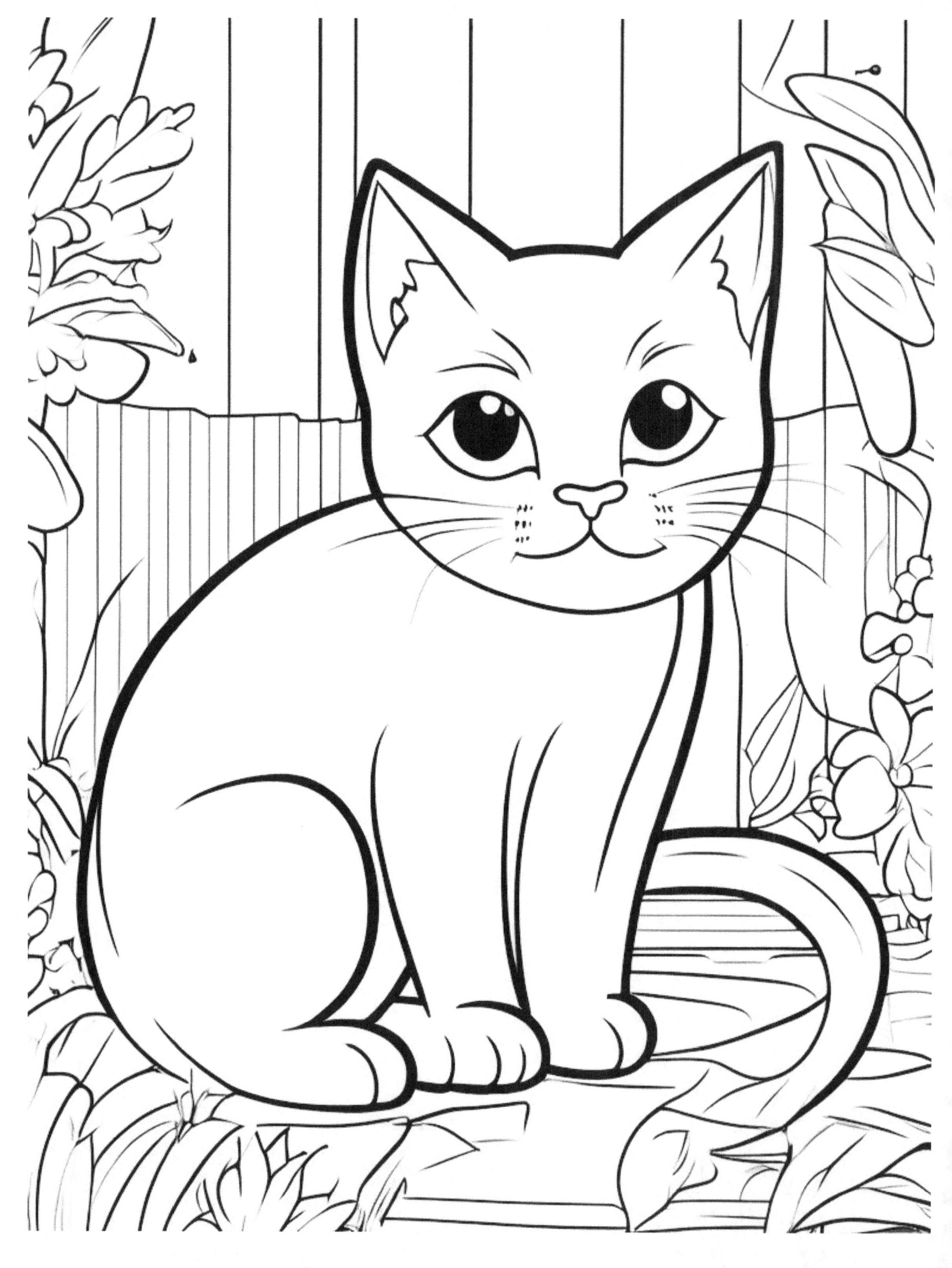

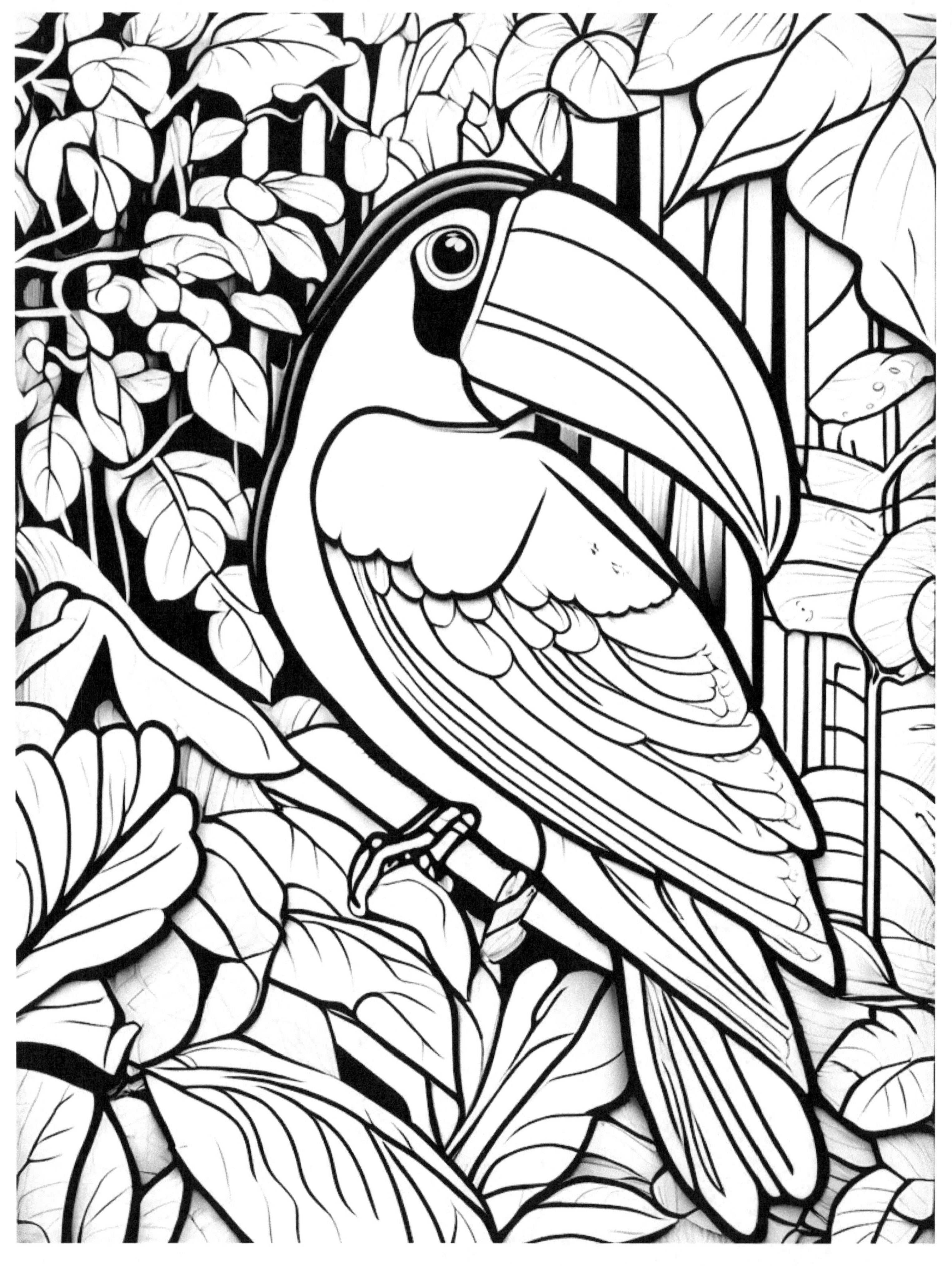

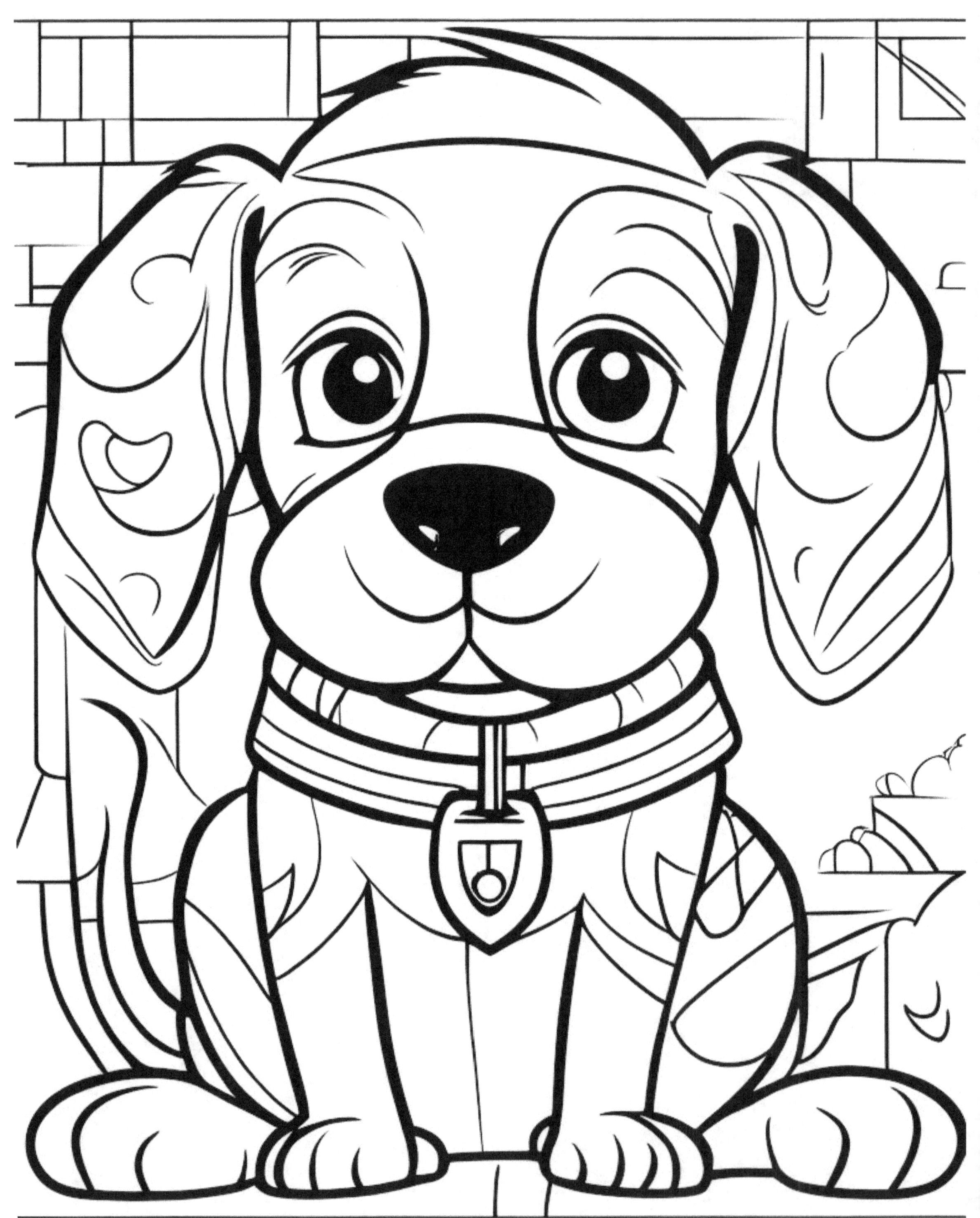

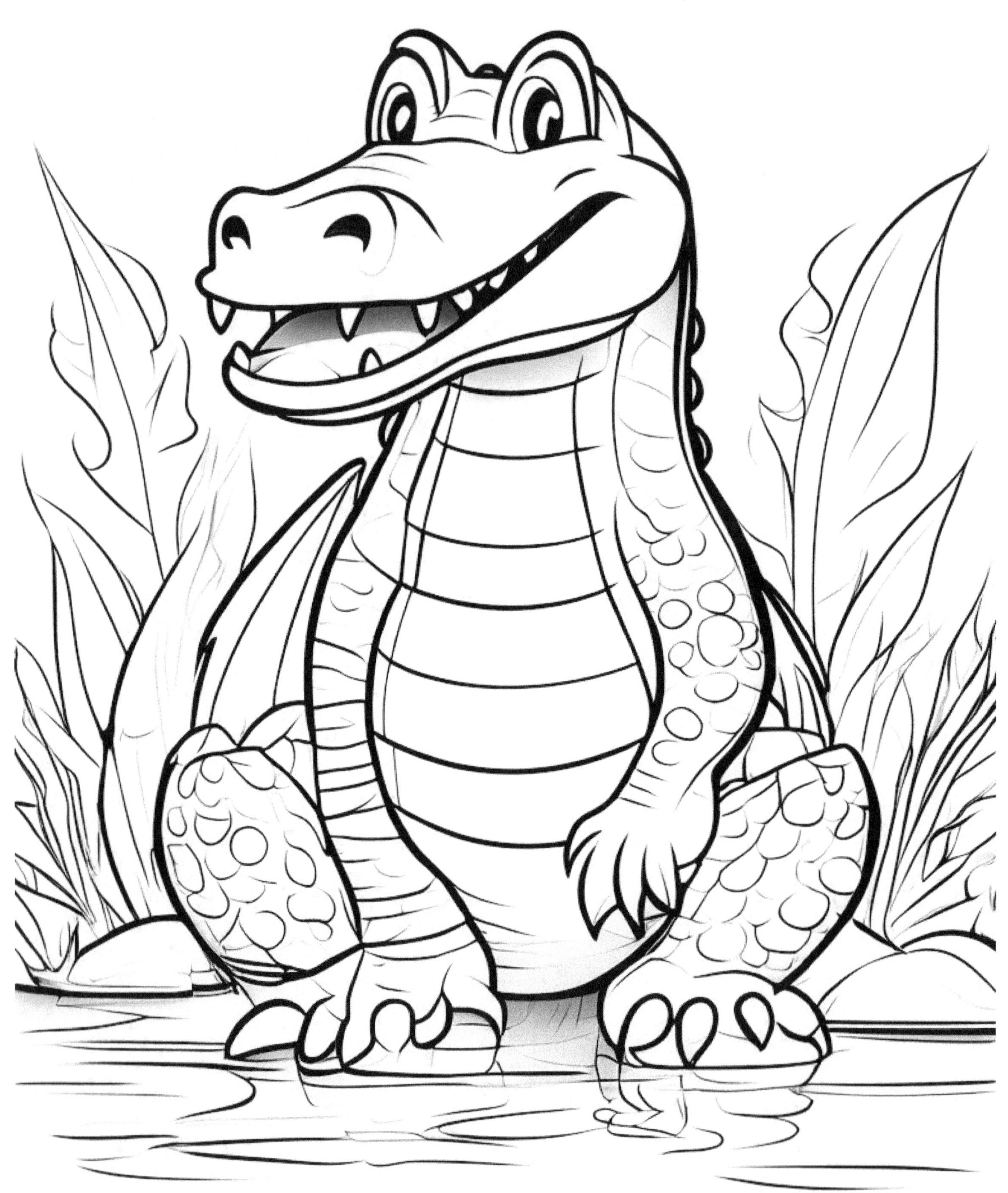

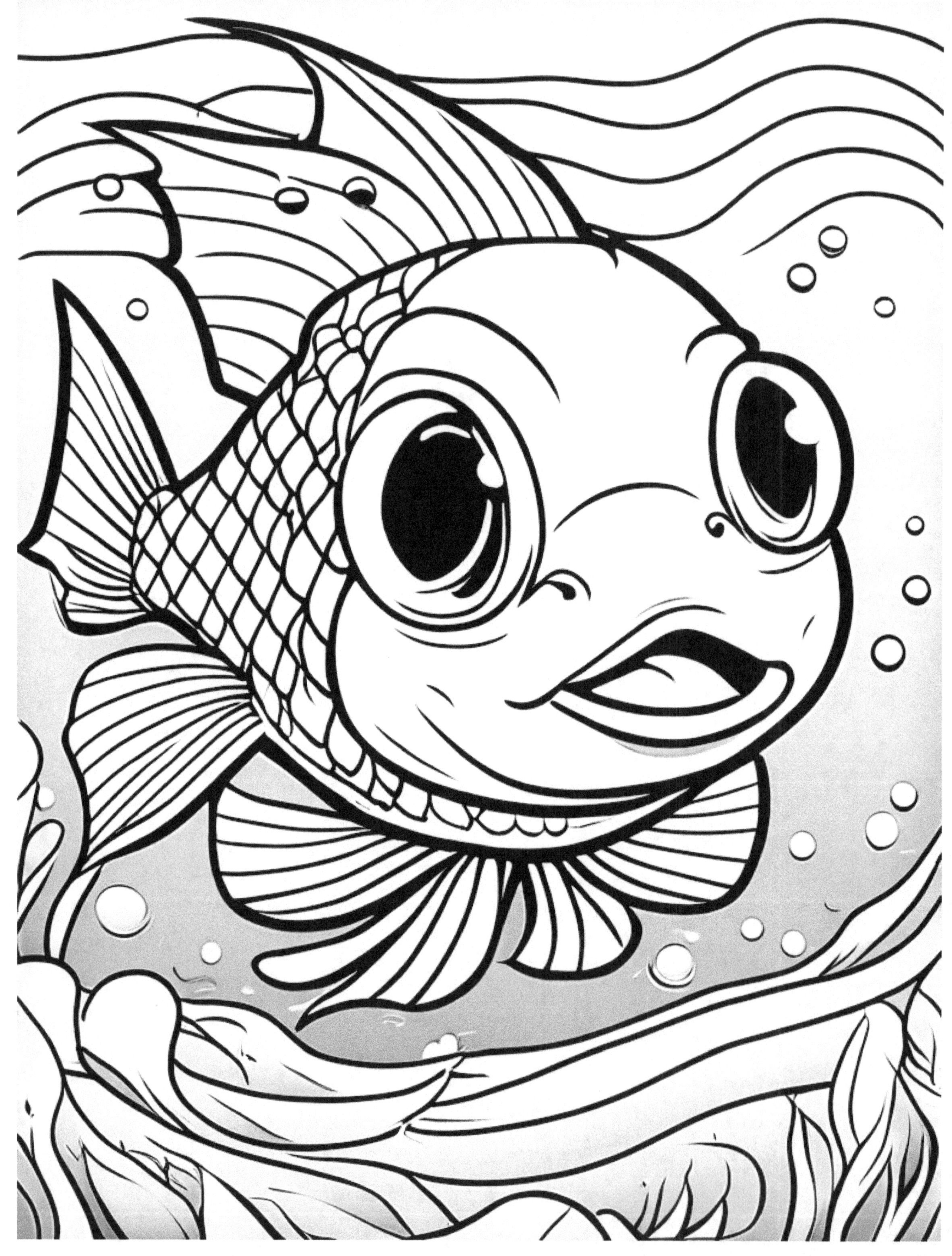